Agency
Amplified

Achieve Scale in a Shifting Digital Landscape

"Success is not final;
failure is not fatal:
It is the courage to
continue that
counts."

– Winston Churchill

Contents

INTRODUCTION

"The range of what we think and do is limited by what we fail to notice. And because we fail to notice that we fail to notice there is little we can do to change until we notice how failing to notice shapes our thoughts and deeds."
- R. D. Laing

Do you know what needs to be done for your agency but struggle with the *how?* Maybe you've combed through Facebook groups, spoken to a few consultants, or even read a few e-books, some of which were nothing more than clickbait. I've been there, and I know it's pretty darn frustrating. As an agency owner, I understand the struggles of developing workflows, improving efficiencies, and ultimately scaling my agency. Finding success in all those areas depended on learning what not to do. While I believe we need to fail forward until we succeed, learning from others' mistakes can save you from a world of pain.

In this book, you'll learn from the mistakes I made in my career as president of a boutique construction insurance agency, Goodman Insurance Services, based out of California. I am not just a consultant or a coach. I am a practitioner at heart and still oversee the day-to-day operations at my agency, which requires having a pulse on the current struggles of agency owners. I am also (proudly) a nerd, not the typical producer type who wines and dines or networks at every available event. I earn business through my ability to problem-solve and understand policy forms better than anyone else. By the age of twenty-nine, I was named one of the top five construction specialists in the nation by *Risk and Insurance Magazine* and featured in several insurance publications for my ability to systematize insurance operations.

But I didn't do all this alone. My brother and business partner worked alongside me every step of the way. A couple of years ago, he and I launched Total CSR, a course that has since trained over ten thousand insurance professionals. Our work puts us in constant contact with CEOs from across the country to discuss strategy, operations, and technology challenges, and it's through this lens that I have written this book.

But this book is not about me. It is about you, your agency, and the operational excellence you can achieve when you take planned action. My experiences, particularly the difficulties I've faced, will help you avoid the same burnt-out systems that prevent your agency from reaching its full potential. The systems and information shared in this book are relevant to the challenges you face today and those your agency will face tomorrow.

Successfully managing your people, systems, processes, and data has seemingly become more complicated in recent years. Buzzwords like *insurtech*, *KPIs*, *churn*, and many others dominate the social media world and flow incessantly from consultants' and product salesmen's mouths.

Meanwhile, agency owners are trying to build client-centric business models that fully leverage today's technology. Effectively building this model while not driving your team mad may seem like a herculean task. Don't worry, I've got you covered.

This book is designed to help agency owners tackle the above issues and own their role as industry leaders. If you use this book to positively contribute to change in your organization, your entire team and the industry at large will be better for it. I have also included the top fifty questions insurance professionals ask me in part 2 of this book. And for the industry newbies, I have specifically included two bonus chapters at the end of this book that will serve as a roadmap from moving beyond a novice to an absolutely indispensable member of your agency.

So how do agencies tackle all the challenges above? Head-on. Let's get started.

Running a profitable agency isn't easy, especially in today's competitive marketplace. But with strategic planning and effective implementation of specific profit-driven processes, it can be done with great success. Top-performing agencies stand out among competitors mainly because they effectively focus on five key foundational areas: vision, people, systems, process, and data. Truly great agencies aim for clear targets and skillfully leverage the right people in the right positions to accomplish goals. They systemize every aspect of their business and build processes that support amazing customer experiences. And finally, they know exactly how to leverage data to gain strategic insight that informs operational decisions. Allow me to elaborate on these five foundational principles and illustrate a roadmap for execution in your agency.

Vision

The moment you begin your career in the insurance sector, your vision must be tied to tangible future goals—goals that connect with and motivate your team members. A strong vision statement illustrates clear values and goals. It doesn't borrow from someone else's dreams or place burdens on your staff. But ultimately, your vision must be clearly communicated and adopted throughout your entire organization. If team members can't get behind it, they don't belong in your organization.

Your vision should drive and motivate your staff with a foundational purpose that is specific and directional. An effective vision includes standards of excellence and definitions of what your company's customer experience should look like. When team members can visualize results, engagement and motivation increases. As a result, they become part of the vision—taking ownership of it.

This ownership inspires employees to become more adept at monitoring themselves, which makes the overall vision more attainable thanks to the internal motivation coming from everyone involved. And so, whenever possible, vision should be communicated through all content coming out of your organization—whether meant for clients, partners, or employees. After all, when everyone understands what your organization is trying to accomplish, the work becomes easier all around. Vendor partners will work in conjunction with you to achieve goals. And clients will double as unpaid consultants, eagerly offering crucial information and suggestions for ways you can improve service.

People

The second area to focus on is people. It goes without saying that it's imperative to recruit the right people for the right roles. A good cultural fit is not enough. Team members' skills must align with what's required for success in each position. In addition, the people you hire should embody your core values and demonstrate their commitment to your agency's vision through their work. To do this, employees must understand the expectations of their roles through proper onboarding and robust training programs. Even the best hires will never adopt your organizational culture and goals without training. Successful agencies leverage both mentoring and cross-training—often charging Millennials and Gen-Zers to assist older employees with technology adoption. In contrast, older and more seasoned employees share their experience, expertise, and industry-based knowledge. Through this synergy, the customer experience is inevitably enhanced, leading to higher retention ratios. Agencies that are effective in this area ultimately become recruitment magnets for talented individuals interested in fulfilling careers, rather than simply jobs. And the loyalty you build means that your best talent is much less likely to turnover.

Systems

The next critical focus is systems, which must be chosen and implemented to support all of the aforementioned parameters. To succeed today, agencies must integrate technology that furthers operational efficiencies while serving the best interest of customers. Agency management systems should support customized proposal templates based on niche focus and coverage lines. Without this, agencies will pay a premium for glorified word processors who will wind up spending more time typing proposal details—time they could be using to guide clients. Remember, it's not enough to simply implement systems, you must make sure that your employees fully adopt them. Failure to do so negates any efficiency gains. So, if you're not committed to fully implementing technology, don't bother investing in it.

The right system improvements will generate predictable client experiences—essential to success in today's customer-centric world. Incorporating better systems can reduce redundant manual tasks and allow your team to focus on providing better experiences. Plus, through efficiency gains, you'll free up capital for sales and marketing efforts.

Process

Great processes are essentially consistent and repeatable experiences—the final focus we'll discuss here. Ask yourself these questions: Does your company have a specific process for each action? Are the processes systematized? Are the operations process-driven, ensuring every individual is aware of their responsibilities? Does everyone understand their roles? Once established, your company's processes should be documented in written and video format. Remember to update documentation and procedures when software updates necessitate changes. And don't forget to ensure that your onboarding includes introductions and clear explanations of all essential procedures and processes. Eliminating ambiguities shuts down potential excuses for performance issues before they arise.

Once you establish your processes, it's important to estimate the amount of time it should take to complete each action item. This information will become critical data for future decision-making.

Data

Is there information available regarding the quote-to-bind ratio by producer and lead source on new business? Do you know the expenses associated with acquiring a new piece of business? Understanding the return on investment will guide your long-range planning and ensure that resources are appropriately allocated.

Leveraging data will enable you to reward team members who contribute to your agency's success. Rewarding employees for their results-oriented performance will increase the likelihood that they will want to continue producing, further driving a consistent experience for your customers while ushering a more predictable top-line growth. Detailed data points also make it easier to identify breakdowns related to systems, people, and processes. With reliable data, most issues very quickly become clear, increasing the likelihood of a quick resolution when problems do arise.

Next Steps

Throughout this book, we will cover many of these areas in greater detail to provide a roadmap with actionable steps you can implement in your agency. We begin with your people.

PART 1:
AMPLIFYING YOUR PEOPLE, SYSTEMS AND PROCESSES

CHAPTER 1:
FINDING TALENT
IN AN INSURANCE DESERT

"Acquiring the right talent is the most important key to growth. Hiring was - and still is - the most important thing we do."

— **Marc Bennioff**, Founder, Chairman and co-CEO of Salesforce

Insurance agencies are being pinched by a tight labor market, an aging workforce, and a series of demographic and cultural challenges with the workforce now available for hire. Put simply, agencies are losing workers faster than they can replace them, and competition for new talent is at an all-time high.

If you own an agency that needs to hire new professionals to replace workforce turnover, you know the pressure is high. Between workers retiring and others leaving to pursue opportunities elsewhere, you might doing more hiring now than at any time in the past twenty years. If you're having problems finding qualified employees, you might even be tempted to hire any warm body that applies.

But you should never make important hiring decisions out of desperation. Instead, there are five proven steps you can take to make sure you're getting the best talent available. By following these guidelines, you'll find, hire, and keep the best possible talent for your agency.

1. Hire for Attitude and Aptitude.

When seeking potential candidates, many companies scour their networks to find anyone with relevant work history and a good reference from someone they know. But hiring a great candidate should be much more scientific than just looking for a connection to someone known to you. A better way to ensure your candidates are really a fit for your organization is to look at their attitude and their aptitude.

Attitude can be fairly subjective, but the right mix of attitude traits for an insurance agency customer sales rep is easy to spot. Consider these questions as you evaluate a candidate's application:

1. Will their attitude "fit" with the other employees in your professional setting?

2. Is the candidate enthusiastic about the role?

3. Do they appear motivated and inspire confidence that they'll show up to work and do a good job?

4. Are they self-aware enough to be a team player and understand that they need to learn from others? Are they eager to learn?

If the candidate is a hard no on any of these questions, it might be a sign that they don't have the right attitude for the role.

For a more scientific approach, utilize services that help you determine which personality traits are most important for certain roles. Identify your best CSR and contract with a company like Total CSR to evaluate them with a personality profile. Then you can match candidates against your employee's personality profile to find positive matches. A candidate with a personality that matches a known successful employee is a great sign that your candidate has the traits to also succeed in that role.

Aptitude can be even more objective. In addition to the standard indicators like test scores and grade point averages, you can also use companies like Total CSR to evaluate intelligence and critical thinking skills. They can help you design and administer tests to identify critical cognitive skills in your applicants. With a third-party service like this, you can sort through your applicants to identify prospects with advantages in key cognitive abilities and even help you find candidates that you might otherwise have overlooked.

2. Don't Be Afraid to Look Outside the Industry for New Employees

One of the core challenges facing insurance agencies is that the pool of qualified candidates with experience in the industry and who are looking for jobs in the industry is limited. One great way to expand the available talent pool, however, is to reach outside the industry for prospects with the right skill set.

Identifying the right skill set isn't as challenging as it might seem, and once you know it, you'll have the information you need to hire professionals with or without industry experience.

Often this means looking for the right skills in nontraditional places. For example, the skills to be a successful insurance customer sales rep are needed for many customer-facing roles, whether in sales, customer service, or another job. Potential candidates are likely all around you.

If you come across someone who stands out and shows their skills in a different setting, you may want to consider how those skills could morph into a successful insurance career—then hire that person! The keys to success are in looking for the right skills in people you meet and being ready to take action when you find them.

3. Leverage Learning Development Trends

After hiring, you'll need a robust onboarding program to help new hires acquire the job-specific skills they need to be successful. I talk about this more in the next chapter, but this detail is key in finding new hires, especially those outside the insurance industry. As author Cameron Bishop wrote it in his 2018 *Forbes* article "Seven Learning and Development Trends to Adopt in 2019," employers should "View training as an employee benefit and bait for talent acquisition." Bishop goes on to say

Training can be a key differentiator between companies competing for talent. Employees want to work for organizations that provide personal and professional development, and they consider it a deciding factor when looking for new employment or determining if they should stay with their current employer. . . . Leverage your training as an employee incentive, and add it to your existing benefits package alongside retirement and health and wellness options.

Bishop equates training to other, more "traditional" employee benefits, even if many companies do not.

Companies routinely consider paid time off, retirement plans, and similar benefits to be significant perks. They list these benefits prominently during the hiring process, yet many don't put training opportunities in this same category. For the companies that offer training to employees, not advertising this information to potential hires is a missed opportunity.

With many companies lagging behind in employee education, effective training and continuing learning opportunities are both great perks to highlight during a competitive hiring process. Furthermore, learning opportunities are great tools to keep your employees engaged and up to date on industry best practices, helping them feel valued and perform at a high level.

4. Offer a Different Career Roadmap

Human resources (HR) professionals often talk about an employee roadmap—a list of milestones an employee meets while at a company.

The traditional employee roadmap is often portrayed as a segment of road that represents the "path" an employee takes while working for you. HR teams look at important points along the way, or "moments that matter," and call them out as stops or turns on the employee's roadmap.

Every employee has an onboarding experience, a variety of career changes along the way, and finally an offboarding experience when the employee's path and the company's diverge. But what happens to an employee's career while they're on "your road" is something you can influence.

The typical insurance agency career roadmap doesn't have many twists and turns. Often an employee will start in customer service and stay in the job for several years. Their only changes may be becoming an agent or deciding to leave your agency to pursue a new opportunity.

But the insurance industry has many career paths, and training, continued learning, and professional certifications offer great ways for young professionals to advance their careers. Offering alternate plans for your employees to advance their careers can help you attract employees with varied interests and help you retain employees with valuable skills who want to make a professional change. What's good for them is good for your agency.

5. Consider Students

Every professional, even the most successful and most talented, started off as an unproven beginner with zero experience. At any given time, there is a whole ecosystem of potential superstars toiling away at local colleges and universities, looking for any opportunity to get some real-world work experience.

Many college students will go so far as to take unpaid internships, trading their effort for experience they can put on their resumes. Others can't work for free but would jump at the chance to trade part-time jobs waiting tables or doing manual labor for an office job that pays and provides professional experience.

The enthusiasm college students have about this kind of work experience, however, comes with important caveats. They may only have limited hours to give, their turnover rates may be high, and even the good ones might not ever take a full-time job in the industry.

That said, a student hire might be very effective as a part-time employee and give you quality service for the next couple of years. And if you ultimately find someone who is a great fit, they may be eager to become a long-time employee after graduation.

Even student employees who aren't stellar themselves can become great recruiters for you among their peers. They might find their work with you rewarding and speak about it in their network of recent and pending college graduates. An endorsement from a peer might just be how you find your next superstar employee.

The End Result

It's a tough time to be an insurance agency with a need to hire, but there are options. Taking even little steps to give yourself an advantage in the hiring process can give you a big advantage in actually landing the talent you want.

Simple tricks, like looking outside the industry and to nontraditional sources to find employees, can help you unearth hidden gems tucked away elsewhere in the workforce. You can also incentivize candidates to apply by providing professional training opportunities that help your employees onboard successfully and develop important skills. Additionally, providing chances for your employees to define their own career roadmaps within your company can help you keep the talent you have and help your agency keep running at top efficiency.

CHAPTER 2:
THE TALENT ASSESSMENT BLUEPRINT

"If you can hire people whose passion intersects with the job, they won't require any supervision at all. They will manage themselves better than anyone could ever manage them. Their fire comes from within, not from without. Their motivation is internal, not external."

— Stephen Covey

The rising use of technology in the hiring process by employers and applicants has significantly lowered the entry barrier for job seekers. A single job posting can now generate hundreds of applicants, leaving agency leaders and HR departments a wealth of choices—perhaps too many. Rather than having too few applicants, many agencies now must comb through a stack (or inbox full) of resumes to find the right candidate.

Separating the good candidates from the bad can be a frustrating, time-consuming process that prohibits employers from carefully reviewing applications. Studies show that most applicants spend less than two minutes reading the job description. Consequently, many applicants often fail to meet the minimum requirements for a job. As the need to weed out these applications grows, HR departments need ways to efficiently differentiate a good application from a bad one—otherwise, bad applicants may make their way to the interview stage while more-qualified candidates are erroneously passed over.

The best agencies know how to make a fully informed decision about whether a candidate is a good or bad hire. They know the solutions available to streamline the hiring process. By utilizing better preemployment technology, agencies can save themselves time, money, and a lot of exhaustive effort.

In this chapter, I talk about what preemployment tests are, what they do, the benefits they provide to agencies and their potential new hires, and how to best use preemployment tests to bring about optimal results.

What Are Preemployment Tests?

Preemployment tests are tools an employer can use to collect pertinent data from potential hires in an objective and standardized way. Quality tests are created by professionals, reviewed thoroughly, and provide an efficient and effective way for employers to prescreen applicants for critical capabilities and traits. A preemployment test may even provide insight into the level of productivity to expect from a potential new hire.

There is a wide selection of preemployment tests available, but most tests will fall into three categories:

1. Aptitude
2. Personality
3. Skills

Let's take a moment to look at the purpose of each of these three tests.

Aptitude Tests

Aptitude tests measure critical thinking, problem-solving skills, and the ability to learn, retain, and apply new information. In short, aptitude tests assess an applicant's overall intelligence and brainpower.

Problem-solving skills and the ability to learn and apply new information are particularly critical in the insurance industry. Finding talent that possesses both qualities is a win-win for the employee and the agency's long-term success.

Personality Tests

Personality tests have gained popularity in many companies, but there is still a lot of confusion about what these types of tests measure and how to use them.

At their core, personality tests provide insight into these questions:

1. Will the candidate be comfortable in this role?

2. Does the candidate possess the character and behavioral traits that will lead to success in this role?

The personality test can assess whether a candidate has a behavioral inclination that fits both the position and the agency's culture. There are numerous options as far as the traits that can be measure by this type of test, but most tests follow a five-factor model that evaluates agreeableness, conscientiousness, extroversion, openness, and stress tolerance. These five factors are becoming increasingly popular over the traditional introvert-extrovert, type A–Type B models.

Using a five-factor model gives a broader, more in-depth look at aspects of personalities that paint a better picture of a candidate's fit in a particular role. Effective personality tests can also reduce turnover since they can uncover whether a candidate would be happy and comfortable working in a specific job.

To illustrate this last point, let's look at two roles that exist in every agency: sales and service.

A salesperson is generally going to be assertive and competitive. A service person, on the other hand, needs to be cooperative and patient.

By utilizing the personality test in the hiring process, an agency can identify a match (or mismatch) based on general required personality traits for the role versus those traits the applicant possesses.

Skills Tests

A skills test helps measure specific capabilities needed for the job, such as a candidate's ability to complete an Association for Cooperative Operations Research and Development (ACORD) form. Skills tests can also evaluate insurance knowledge; verbal, math, and communication skills; and typing and computer proficiency.

Candidates may have picked up these skills in school or prior work experience, but they may not always be featured on a resume or be on par with their aptitude. Therefore, a skills test is a great way to assess whether an applicant knows enough to complete the job effectively.

How Can Agencies Benefit from Using Preemployment Tests?

Prescreening employees via tests offers agencies the opportunity streamline the hiring process so it meets their needs. Some agencies may only use tests for certain roles, and others may find great benefits in using preemployment tests uniformly across the organization. Here are some of the improvements to the hiring process that agencies should expect to see.

Time Savings

While there will certainly be serious and qualified applicants for a job, a significant percentage of applicants will need to be filtered out. Whether a job posting generates fifty applicants or over two hundred applicants, that's still a lot of resumes to sift through, even to do just a quick review for red flags. Any person who has spent time in this type of process can attest that the breaking point is just after the first twenty-five resumes.

By adding a preemployment test at the beginning of the process, agencies can quickly eliminate candidates who are not qualified. Agencies will save significant time (and headache) reviewing resumes and reduce the time spent interviewing unqualified applicants. This extra time and energy can then go toward evaluating serious candidates.

Cost Savings

The saying "time is money" applies to the painstaking hiring process. There is a cost associated with every step of recruiting, from the expense of advertising for an open position to the salaries of every person involved in interviewing, extending and negotiating offers, onboarding, and training. The cost of the turnover and the need to reinitiate the hiring cycle further compounds hiring expenses.

The use of preemployment testing narrows the field of candidates at the top of the funnel, meaning fewer resumes require a full review. Even fewer candidates make on to the interview stage. Preemployment testing also provides increased assurance that the right candidate with the right qualifications, aptitude, and personality will be hired, reducing concerns about overall turnover. Both byproducts represent significant cost savings to an agency at all stages of the hiring process.

Less Guesswork

Data continues to be vital to knowing and understanding clients in the insurance industry, but data can also play a crucial role when looking to bring new talent into an organization. Without data, hiring decisions happen based on experience and intuition. While both certainly serve a purpose, relying on preemployment tests helps by providing objective data based on job-specific criteria. Utilizing data removes a significant portion of the guesswork and allows agency leaders to make more-informed decisions.

A Clear Picture of Employee Productivity

It can be hard to judge how effective a job candidate will be based solely on their resume and interview chops. The applicant's goal, after all, is to paint themselves in their best light—but the painting doesn't always match reality.

Preemployment tests can predict a candidates' potential productivity by assessing whether the applicant has the right knowledge, skills, and abilities to perform as expected.

A More Objective Standard

Preemployment tests adhere to federal guidelines, which encourage more equitable and nondiscriminatory hiring processes.

This high level of regulation helps companies maintain a more objective selection process. Generally, tests are less subjective and help reduce bias that can otherwise become an issue during the hiring process.

A well-validated test will not evaluate age, sex, race, or any other criteria that can lead to a suit about unfair hiring practices. As long as tests are created based on job-related skills and traits, a test can provide better defensibility should a suit be brought against the agency.

Implementing Preemployment Testing

Preemployment tests are not an out-of-the-box solution. They require some build-out for the agency to significantly benefit from adding tests to their current hiring process.

Here are the steps that are most critical to making preemployment testing a success.

1. **Job Analysis.** Each role in the agency will need to be reviewed and evaluated to create a thorough job description, which includes the skills, work activities, and abilities required for the job. Based on this information, the selection of test criteria can measure the specific skills, abilities, and personality traits that produce optimal performance in the role.

2. **Decide on Test Relevancy.** After a job is analyzed, leaders can then decide what tests are most pertinent. Perhaps one role requires skills and aptitude tests but not a personality test. Other roles may need all three to assess candidate capabilities accurately. The goal should be to decide which tests best suit the needs of the role and helps agency leaders make the most informed decision while hiring.

3. **Decide When to Test.** Testing early in the hiring process can prevent extra work down the line. It allows hiring managers to collect objective data about candidates and ensure that anyone who makes it to the next stage meets the position's basic skill requirements. Early testing can save significant time and effort that would typically be required to evaluate

an overwhelming number of resumes. There is no wrong answer; it is more a question of consistency and the desired outcome.

4. **Establish Protocol for Remote Testing.** Most likely, candidates are not coming to the office to complete the preemployment test, especially if testing is being required early in the process. Creating written guidelines about how to take the test will help prevent confusion and reduce the candidate's potential for fraudulent activity.

5. **Test Existing Employees.** Administering tests to current employees will help the agency establish scoring guidelines for each role and associated test. While you may be tempted to only test top-performers, it is crucial to test employees of all levels. A broader selection of employee scores can help you to establish more appropriate benchmarking levels for future hires. As a bonus, testing current employees also allows managers to assess current staff and better understand pain points or areas where employees excel.

6. **Establish Scoring Guidelines.** Based on the ranges provided in testing employees in step 5, agency leaders will need to decide on a minimum and maximum acceptable score for each role and associated preemployment test. Scores that are too low can be a reliable indicator of turnover due to poor performance, while scores that are too high can indicate that an employee will be bored or restless and may leave on their own in search of something more challenging.

Additional Evaluation

Preemployment tests can provide significant advantages to agencies during the hiring process, but it is essential to remember that there is no guaranteed solution to avoiding bad hires. An employee may score high and perform poorly, and a candidate that scores low could still be a top performer in the agency.

There is no magic bullet, and agencies must continue to do their due diligence by consistently evaluating the same criteria for applicants, including resumes, interviews, prior experience, education, and any other factors that may be relevant to the role. Preemployment tests are a significant first step and complement the process of reviewing resumes and conducting interviews, but agencies need to maintain realistic expectations, and use tests to improve, not replace, current hiring practices.

Nonetheless, implementing testing can take a substantial amount of friction out of a challenging process by giving agency leaders insight to make more efficient and effective hiring decisions.

CHAPTER 3:
LEVERAGING CULTURE TO FIGHT TURNOVER

"Hire character. Train skill."

— **Peter Schutz**, Porsche

How employees feel about your agency is a hidden key to your agency's success. After all, metrics like profits and topline growth can only be achieved with people—that is, your team—working toward a shared goal.

In recent years, *culture* has become a business-world buzzword, and for good reason. Thriving insurance agencies recognize the value of a positive culture and take a proactive approach to create an attractive environment while driving financial success. Culture goes beyond a mission statement or abstract concept that is called upon when convenient. It is core values tied to specific behaviors that everyone in the organization knows, understands, believes, and lives out in their day-to-day interactions.

Neglecting culture has serious consequences, including the expense of staff turnover. On the other hand, when culture is an area of focus, companies are more likely to maintain current employees and attract top talent. Creating a work environment that fosters a sense of community and belonging invites the collaboration and loyalty that makes an agency effective and an exciting place to work. That said, building a positive company culture requires time and dedication. This chapter will offer practical steps that you can take to start creating an agency that employees want to be a part of.

Regularly Express Affirmation and Appreciation

Employees need to know that those in charge see them as people and not as a number. They need to know that their role within a company is valued and that the work they do is essential and appreciated. This applies to companies of all sizes. Consistent messaging that highlights this from leadership down to all levels of the organization helps build that sense of value and trust between employees and the employer.

Expressing appreciation requires that you take time to get to know your employees. As organizations grow, this can become increasingly difficult, but a system that creates a more personalized work experience is important. Simple tools include employee onboarding surveys, birthday and anniversary messages, and recognition of other personal and professional achievements.

Provide an Emotionally Safe Work Environment

A safe work environment means employees feel confident in their employer and where they belong in the organization. Employees feel comfortable asking for help and admitting when mistakes are made because they see their employer as an advocate. While a supervisor should set expectations, the best ones make it known that they are there to support employees even when things don't go as planned.

Unsafe work environments, on the other hand, are characterized by fear that forces people to struggle in silence. Asking for help or making mistakes might be perceived as a weakness or reason for disciplinary action, and so employees become more concerned with looking like they have all the answers, even when they don't. This creates a stressful work environment for the employee, which cannot be sustained long term.

Furthermore, recognize that work is just one piece of an employee's life. At any given time, an employee may be facing challenges you are not aware of. These issues may impact the employee's relationships and interactions with coworkers or the quality of their work. A deterioration in behavior or the quality of work should be addressed, but sensitively. Opening the conversation by attacking an employee's behavior or performance without first attempting to understand the unknown factors will most likely provoke an employee to get defensive or shut down altogether. For this reason, approach the employee with compassion and empathy. They may not be willing to open up and provide specifics, but letting them know that you are there because you are concerned will help create a sense of ease for the employee and maintain positive communication.

Call Employees to Greatness

As a leader, you have the responsibility and challenge of helping people meet their potential. Inevitably, however, employees can fall short of that mark. Addressing performance or behavior issues can feel uncomfortable, especially if one lacks the inadequate skill set or willingness to confront challenging situations. However, the real discomfort comes when the problem is avoided altogether. What may have started out as a small incident can grow into a chronic and systemic issue if not addressed immediately.

As Brene Brown writes, "Daring leaders who live into their values are never silent about hard things." Lean in to discomfort—everyone will be better off for it in the end. When you are willing to move through the discomfort of confronting an employee and simultaneously display vulnerability, great things happen. You find an opportunity to address behavior, demonstrate empathy, build on your confrontation skills, and develop better communication strategies.

Provide a Framework for Accountability

A strong company culture helps employees see themselves as part of a team. This means that everyone knows they are accountable to the company and its members as well as the established core values and behaviors. As you all work toward a shared goal, no one has exempt status or receives special treatment. A well-built system of accountability is the foundation for creating trust in an organization. It will also provide a way for individuals to develop better communication and problem-solving skills in the long run. Knowing that everyone is being held to the same standard and playing by the same rules creates clarity for employees.

Provide Consistent Communication

As an organization grows, communicating with each employee becomes increasingly more challenging. The day-to-day operations can become all-consuming, sparking the tendency to share only "big news" rather than providing a constant feed of information. However, if information is not provided from the right source, the door is left wide open for gossip and a churning rumor mill. This type of activity is not only damaging to the culture of an agency, but also leads to lost productivity.

Influential leaders should provide a continuous stream of current information on what is going on with the company. This might include regular updates on company metrics and performance, the status of goals, upcoming changes, and more. They level of transparency helps prevent employees from feeling as though information is being withheld behind closed doors.

The need for better communication, however, cannot be one-sided from leadership down to the rank and file. The best companies create space for two-way conversations. They establish a feedback loop where employees feel comfortable getting and giving information.

Effective communication establishes a connection between the company, its leadership, and its employees. It fosters relationship building and helps everyone in the organization become better communicators. When employees are active participants in the conversation, they can better understand their role in the company, which ultimately leads to better employee retention.

Provide Opportunities to Build Deeper Relationships

Finding connection and support in those you work closely with adds value to the work experience, especially during intense or stressful periods. While remote employees may not have the pleasure of working the same room as their team, creating opportunities (even virtual ones) for employees to get to know one another and build connections can foster belonging and team spirit.

When teams are not given space to get to know one another, the disconnect between team members prevents individuals from working together as effectively as they could. Employees don't feel as welcome or may feel neglected entirely, almost as if they are not part of the team at all. Taking steps to break down those feelings of isolation will yield dividends with employee performance.

The use of video in remote meetings is a simple but key way to make a virtual gatherings feel more personal. Video conferencing allow everyone a chance to see one another even when they can't be in the same room and can help generate better connections. When teams build stronger connections, they communicate more effectively. Simon Sinek notes that "This feeling of belonging, of shared values and a deep sense of empathy, dramatically increases trust, cooperation and problem solving."

Encouraging socializing between employees is another great way for your teams to build stronger relationships with one another. While some of this naturally happens during the workday, encouraging additional ad-hoc conversation, even through messaging software if working remotely, can keep the team connected throughout the day.

Finally, support efforts for events outside of the office, whether it is attending a sporting event, a company picnic, dinner at a local establishment, or any number of activities. The options are endless. Most important is finding activities that are enjoyable to everyone and encourage the whole group to participate.

Invest in Employee Growth

Employees who are satisfied with working the same job for their entire career are rare. For most, knowing there are opportunities to continue learning and growing increases how satisfied they feel about their work. When employees don't feel encouraged to learn and explore, there is a good chance they will find their way to another organization that is more receptive to their ambitions.

Employees want to broaden their skill sets, take on new challenges, and explore different options in their field—or maybe another line of work altogether. This is a good thing, and employers should view lifelong learning as a "skill in and of itself that will forward careers as it contributes to your company's innovative prospects," writes Chris Dyer, CEO of PeopleG2. Providing employees space to experiment with different responsibilities and learning opportunities adds value to the employer-employee relationship.

While getting to know your employees, be sure to understand their talents and interests. Keep an open dialogue about what they want in a career and what education or tools they need to reach their current and future roles. Allow employees to take the initiative and be a promotor of their continued success. Leaders must be there to encourage and challenge their employees to learn new skills and continuously level up—even if it means the employee eventually leaves for a more fitting opportunity outside of their current organization.

The Cost of Inaction

When agencies do not invest in building a healthy workplace culture, it will cost them in the long run. Failure to dedicate time and other resources to creating or improving all aspects of company culture will prevent an organization from growing in all the ways that it could. The biggest expense will be the loss of employee satisfaction, which ultimately leads to staff turnover.

A recent Gallup article estimated the cost of turnover to US businesses at one trillion dollars per year, with an overall turnover rate of 26.3 percent. Replacing an employee takes time, and the cost amounts to about 2.5 months of their salary, as noted in *Talent and Training Challenges Facing Insurance Agencies* in 2019. Even a small company with ten employees can experience significant turnover cost.

The good news is that the turnover problem can be corrected and prevented when a company gets intentional about building a culture that retains good employees. Winning on culture is the cornerstone to allowing an agency to succeed.

When a company is known as being a great place to work both inside and outside of the organization, everyone wins.

CHAPTER 4:
RADICAL ACCOUNTABILITY

"Leaders inspire accountability through their ability to accept responsibility before they place blame."

— **Courtney Lynch**

Accountability is one of the biggest challenges in business, and insurance agencies are no exception. Accountability (or lack thereof) will impact every aspect of an agency's operations. It's the pacesetter for everything else that happens. Lack of accountability is the most significant factor in determining whether an agency achieves its growth objectives.

Developing and successfully implementing a plan to achieve your agency's growth objectives is contingent upon how effective the organization is at holding itself accountable. Agency-wide accountability standards ensure that all parts of the organization are working together to achieve the same goal. Unfortunately, workplace accountability surveys show that 93 percent of employees don't understand the vision or even the strategic goals of the company where they work. Seventy percent of that same group stated they also don't understand how the organization measures success.

So how do you create accountability within your agency? This playbook will provide valuable insight into building great accountability in your operation by focusing on the *why*, *what*, *who*, *when*, and *where*.

The Why

The *why* is the most critical part of the puzzle. It maps to the company vision and serves as the foundation of accountability within the agency. It is the guide for all decisions, and the results of those decisions will feed back into the why.

If, for example, the vision of the company is significant growth within the region achieved by attaining 15 percent net revenue growth year over year, then all actions within the agency should ultimately support that specific strategic goal.

The why will dictate *what* action needs to take place at every level of the organization to achieve that growth goal. The why will be the driver behind the tasks that need to happen and the processes that need to be built and changed to better align with the company vision. It will provide clarity on what results are achieved when each step is executed as designed.

It will validate the purpose of each role in the company—the *who*—and the impact those roles have on the vision of the company. Having an individual to monitor, analyze, and report on key performance indicators (KPIs) will be critical to making sure the organization moving toward its goals. This also serves to identify parts of a process that are negatively impacting performance.

The why is also the reference point for *how* the organization will address processes that need to change to help the agency align with the company vision.

It informs *when* performance needs to be analyzed. When is the information necessary to ensure the agency is on pace for the desired growth? When is this information most critical to being able to act on it?

And as the agency continues to grow, evolve, and move closer to the goal, employees will adopt the vision or find a different organization to join. The why keeps everyone involved by setting the standard for *where* communication takes place to keep employees engaged.

In short, the why is what pulls everything together. It is the catalyst for all decisions, changes, and processes within the agency to achieve the corporate vision.

The What

The *what* focuses on actions or specific tasks that go on in an agency to continue moving the organization towards the company vision. It is represented in every process within the agency. It is deliberate and intentional, providing clear direction on what action needs to happen and when to maintain forward momentum. It also serves as a trail of breadcrumbs when other things come along that distract team members from their responsibilities.

It is critical that information about the what is communicated thoroughly. Team members need to know what steps need to be taken hourly, daily, weekly, monthly, and quarterly and what is required to make all those steps work together for the benefit of the agency. When executed well, it eliminates ambiguity and creates a clear roadmap for success.

For example, when a submission needs to get out to market, what steps need to happen to ensure that the process is completed successfully? Here is an example process.

What Comprises a Complete Submission

This will list all the required information that needs to be gathered and will include information such as vehicle, driver, payroll and sales information, supplemental applications, currently valued loss runs, ex-mod worksheets, and updated ACORD applications.

What Must Happen

This part of the process will outline the steps that are required to make sure that all necessary parts of the submission are accounted for. It will include details on what each person involved in the process is responsible for.

What a Proper Submission Looks Like

Every agency needs a best-in-class submission sample that illustrates the required documents to be included along with a sample of correspondence used when transmitting the submission.

What Tools Are Needed to Accomplish Each Task

Everyone in the agency needs to know what tools are utilized to create and distribute a submission. For instance, email should be used for requesting updated information from the client, loss runs might be requested via email or pulled from online carrier websites, and the agency management system should be used to update ACORD forms.

What Amount of Time Is Required

If the overall objective is to have all submissions prepared and sent out to market 90 days prior to renewal, what needs to happen leading up to those 90 days? The process should provide details to the employee on what steps are required between 90 to 120 days from the policy expiration to ensure all components of the submission are put together and sent out 90 days from renewal.

What Tool Is Used to Trigger the Process

Whether it's activities within the agency management system or an expiration report that team members review daily, employees must leverage some resource or tool to initiate the process.

The Who

When developing an accountability strategy in your agency, you need to understand the role of the *who*.

The first who you need to identify is the person in charge of monitoring the deliverables—the KPIs. This person should have a deep understanding of the corporate vision and the strategic goals that support it.

The next who to focus on is the person reviewing and auditing the KPI data. That person or persons will need to be able to validate information as well as quickly identify errors that may show up in the KPI reports. They must also have a working knowledge of each department's operations and chokepoints.

Once the monitor and auditor are selected, reporting procedures need to be established. In other words, who is the designated messenger for sharing the KPI data? Whoever shares the information must be able to provide meaning and context for the data in the report. It's also important to know who in the organization this information will be distributed to.

As this information is distributed and explained, there will be times when a report uncovers issues that require corrective measures. The person steering the improvement process, therefore, needs to be an effective communicator capable of facilitating discussion while working through conflict.

The role of all the whos could be filled by one person, such as the chief financial officer or head of operations, or several people depending on the size of the organization. Regardless of how many whos are involved, each person must have proven themselves to be highly accountable, as they now have to monitor, interpret, and report on critical information and help implement strategy for the entire organization.

The How

In the process of building the accountability structure for the agency, the *how* will need to be determined. The how must do the following:

- Provide a process by which KPIs are tracked
- Explain auditing guidelines and KPI verification
- Establish a methodology for identifying and analyzing performance issues
- Establish a process-improvement roadmap

For example, an agency has an organization-wide initiative to increase life insurance sales. To accomplish this, all personal line clients, new and existing, should be asked whether they want a life insurance quote when their new or renewal policy is issued. The client file should be documented to track whether and when the life insurance quote is sent to the client.

How Will the Agency Know Whether This Is Being Done?

Reports need to be pulled monthly in conjunction with regular account audits.

How Is the Data Verified?

The life insurance quote report should be compared against the personal lines renewal expiration list over the same thirty-day time period. Audit checks will uncover agents who did not even attempt to quote a life insurance policy for the insured.

How Are Issues Corrected?

The report will be sent to managers to identify the agents who are not following the procedure. Managers will then need to address the performance issue with the individuals and reiterate the expectation that the agents begin following the established process immediately and outline consequences for failure to improve.

How Are Improvements Communicated?

Rinse, wash, repeat. Successful improvement is praised, while those who fail to improve are held accountable.

In short, the how creates a loop of tracking, auditing, improving, and communicating the performance of individual processes in the pursuit of meeting KPIs.

The When

The *when* is the time factor of accountability. It looks at all the KPIs and determines how often certain KPIs are reviewed. Some KPIs may only need to be looked at quarterly or annually, whereas others need to be examined more frequently. The when is an essential part of understanding the required cadence of each KPI to ensure the timely transmission of information to agency leadership.

For example, an agency has a strategic goal of 15 percent organic revenue growth this year. To monitor progress toward this goal, there are specific KPIs that need to be reviewed and examined at differing intervals.

Weekly

Reviewing a producers' prospecting pipeline weekly will provide the insight needed to confirm he or she is generating enough activity to hit the growth objective.

Monthly

Revenue targets will need to be tracked monthly in order to ensure that individual producers stay on track.

Quarterly

Quote-to-bind ratios might be evaluated quarterly to discover producers who are "practice quoting" and wasting carrier and agency resources in the process. Awareness of this will help producers develop better strategies for qualifying leads.

Annually

If the bucket is leaking due to lost accounts, agency principals need to know where in the organization that is taking place and ultimately identify and resolve its root cause.

The Where

As agency performance is tracked and adjustments are made to improve processes and procedures, employees need to be updated regularly so that they can align their actions with the overall strategy.

It is important to know *where* this information be communicated. Will it be communicated via in-person meetings or even Zoom meetings? How are general announcements made? If this information cannot be provided in person, the agency must consider the employees' preferred communication style. Some employees prefer a text-based version, meaning email will be sufficient. Others prefer receiving information over a video platform, so recording a video update for those employees will be valuable.

As an example, an agency has decided to start using an outsourcing company for certain processes that do not require client interaction. This change might have an impact on staffing and workflows while also providing benefits in efficiency and employee workloads. The leadership must communicate these changes, the benefits, and potential stumbling blocks to employees to create transparency and encourage adoption.

To determine the ideal where for your communication, consider the following options

In-Person Meetings

If logistically possible, having in-person meetings is a great way to communicate with employees. It allows the messenger to see the employees and pick up on body language as the information is delivered. It's also a great way to provide a forum where employees can ask questions and communicate potential concerns.

Email

This can be effective for employees who are readers and like to see all the details in black and white. Email is also a great way to document the communication in a way that employees can easily reference in the future.

Video

Millennials and Gen Z employees are natural consumers of video. They are accustomed to taking in information in this manner, both for learning or for entertainment. Utilizing video is a great way to communicate important announcements to employees. It may help employees better connect with the messenger, as they can see a leader's face and hear their tone of voice.

Employee engagement and information dissemination is critical and best achieved through a multichannel approach. Clear communication ensures accountability measures are understood and respected.

Developing, implementing, and enforcing accountability measures in your agency can be challenging, but it is necessary. Top-down accountability is the only proven way to ensure top-line growth.

CHAPTER 5:
ONBOARDING VIRTUAL TEAMS

"We reinforce our culture every chance we get. Our Business Principles are at the forefront of everything we do, and we need to make these principles part of every major conversation at the company – from the hiring, onboarding and training of new recruits to town halls and management meetings to how we reward and incentivize our people."

— **James Dimon** - CEO JP Morgan Chase

Mastering the onboarding process has been an ongoing struggle in insurance agencies as long as the industry has been around. Even with new technology and guidelines around every corner, it has become more challenging to create an ideal experience. Multiple generations are coming into the industry and, often, there is a significant generation gap between the individual managing the onboarding process and the new hire.

Delivering a consistent onboarding experience is challenging, even for the most experienced agencies. They struggle to manage constant changes with HR requirements, new technology used to assist the onboarding process, hardware and software set up, etc. Even the most diligent onboarding checklist users often miss an item or two during the process. Taking onboarding a step further to feel personalized without losing much-needed consistency can feel overwhelming.

Adding the element of managing the entire process remotely, and things start to get more complicated quickly. As remote work becomes the norm in many agencies, and, at the very least, an option for new hires, onboarding becomes a new challenge altogether. The process requires even more rework and creativity to overcome the hurdles presented in a virtual environment versus in-person.

While we will focus on the virtual onboarding process throughout this book, many vital elements apply for both in-person and remote hiring.

Prepare for New Hires with a Robust Pre-Boarding Process

This risk of employees feeling disconnected from the onset is higher in a virtual setup. To ensure this doesn't happen with new hires in your agency, getting an early start on the process is essential to achieving desired onboarding results.

Preboarding includes the steps agencies need to take before the employee's first day and are critical to the success of Day 1:

Technology & Supplies

HR, IT, and the Hiring Manager should know what technology is necessary for the new employee to do their job on Day 1. Assumptions about equipment, internet, phone, etc. can leave a new hire without the essentials, which can, in turn, leave them feeling a little lost from the start. Creating a checklist of all items that need to be purchased, programmed, and shipped will keep all parties on the same page.

Paperwork

The hiring process requires new hires to complete form after form. While a new hire would complete many of these forms on the first day in the past, there is no reason to not take care of them ahead of time. Creating a clean and clear onboarding paperwork packet in an electronic format once the offer is accepted will allow the new hire to get this out of the way during the pre-boarding time frame. It will also allow HR to get all documentation reviewed and handle any details that require clarification before the first day. This preparation will ensure that all the employee data is in the system and only needs review and verification sparing everyone from managing this task during what should be a more engaging and exciting first day.

Welcome Message

A brief welcome email to the new hire when they accept the position can be a great way to get them excited about the new opportunity they will be exploring with your agency in just a couple of weeks. The message should include:

- Introduction of the hiring manager who they will be working with

- Appreciation for their trust in your agency

- What to expect in the coming weeks, whether it is computer equipment or technicians who will be arriving at their residence to set up their office, and any other communication they may receive from the agency or other affiliates

- Required paperwork (as noted above)

- A checklist of items they will need to take care of before Day 1

- A New Hire questionnaire to get a feel for their personality and preferences

- Contact information for agency personnel they can reach if questions or concerns come up along the way

If this feels like a lot for one email, consider breaking it up into a series throughout the days and weeks leading up to the first day.

On the other side of this, is the need for internal communication. The hiring manager should send an all office email announcing the new hire. Even though employees will not be interacting in the same way they would in a traditional office set up, this is not a step you will want to skip. Instead, let other employees know who is starting and what role they will be filling the agency. This information will help everyone remain connected with what is going on within the agency, even in a remote work environment.

New Employee Gift

A gift basket does not need to be anything elaborate or over the top. Consider including a few items such as:

- Favorite snacks (noted on their new hire questionnaire)
- Gift card for a local restaurant (no need to worry about prepping dinner at the end of the first day, the agency has it covered)
- A few necessary office supplies
- Business Cards
- Agency swag like a hat, t-shirt, or blanket

Combining these items pulls together their personal favorites, necessities, and the agency brand, which builds connection and loyalty from the very start.

Emphasize Culture in a Remote Onboarding

Defining culture can be a challenge for many agencies. Translating it from within the traditional office setup to a virtual environment adds a new element. Trying to express all of that to a new hire can feel borderline impossible. Even giant companies like Google have struggled to transition as a company that thrived on their in-office offerings to remote work environments. However, as hard as it may seem, there are ways to help share agency culture beyond in-person interactions and welcome new hires at the same time.

As you are working on preparing for your new hire's first day, put together a personalized welcome video from the agency owner, their manager, and any other team members they will be working with.

- Welcome the employee by name

- Provide a brief history

- Explain the Mission and Values of the agency

- Describe how their role contributes to the goals of the agency

- Include a virtual tour of the agency office if it is an option. Even if they won't be working in the office in the short or long run, providing them an opportunity to experience the office environment can help them build a connection to the agency.

Having a welcome video land in the employee inbox first thing on the first day will provide an excellent way for them to begin engaging with the agency's culture.

Connect Your New Hire with Co-Workers Starting Day 1

Facilitating virtual meetings will be an essential component of communication and help your new hire get to know their way around the agency. Providing as many opportunities as possible to help a new employee make those connections from the start will make a significant difference in how quickly and easily they start to get comfortable with their coworkers and their role.

One on One Meetings

Your new hire's first day should include a couple of one on one meetings. One of the most important is that which takes place between the hiring manager and the individual. This meeting is crucial as it may be one of the first opportunities the new hire has to get to know their supervisor outside of the interview process. During this meeting, the manager will want to:

- Ensure the employee has everything they need as far as equipment and supplies

- Discuss work and training schedules, expectations, and goals

- Review check-in protocols

- Address questions and concerns the employee has

A meeting between the hew hire and HR may be necessary as well. This meeting will be a time to go over any additional paperwork or other pending HR matters, collect signatures and forms, etc. HR can also address any questions the employee has during this meeting.

Team Meetings

Generating team interactions from the beginning will be critical to for the new hire to begin building relationships with the team they will be working with. "Gather" the group together using the meeting software of choice. Make sure everyone is on camera. If possible, schedule the meeting in a more relaxed format, perhaps as a "coffee break" style meeting or even during lunch. This meeting allows the new hire to see and familiarize themselves with each person on the team.

Providing an opportunity for a new employee to put a name with a face and a voice will help break the ice and establish a higher comfort level when working with and asking questions of other individuals in the future.

Set the Employee up for Long Term Success

Providing the tools and information the employee needs to start off on the right foot is important on that first day. It helps the employee feel more connected and settles those first day jitters. However, creating a solid plan for their development over the weeks and months to follow is just as important to their long-term success with the agency.

Training

Training is critical to any new hire's success, but the fallout of getting it wrong in a remote onboarding situation is much higher. Creating a solid training plan becomes even more imperative when the opportunities to clarify understanding require more effort with the trainer and trainee.

Training starts with a well-written job description. Ensure the role is ultra-clear. The confusion caused by ambiguity can be even more destructive in a virtual environment. A new hire may be nervous about pressing for clarification which puts the employee at risk for disengaging early on.

- Individual goals need to be clearly defined, as well. Ensure the employee understands the expectations and how they should be progressing in their training. Whether through coverage and process quizzes, activity reports, or trainer feedback, leaving these things in the unknown can be unsettling to a new hire. Also, be sure to document all the details, and that both the manager and employee know where to access it.

- Knowing in-person training is not an option in the immediate future, agencies must use technology to redesign and modernize training. Paper-heavy processes guides no longer work. Digitizing workflows into centrally-located PDF's is a minimum standard. Creating video tutorials for workflows and processes is the best way to provide step by step instructions a new hire can easily reference and repeat as needed. A combination of recorded tutorials, digitized workflows, and virtual training sessions will help connect all of the dots.

Teamwork

As mentioned earlier, helping a new hire connect with their team will be essential for them to establish a comfort level within the agency and with their role. The more comfortable they are with the group, the more willing they will be to ask questions that will undoubtedly come up along the way.

One of the best ways to help a new hire integrate with the agency and with their team is to assign a mentor. This person ideally has experience in the same role, is familiar with the technology options for communication, will stay in touch with the mentee, and is a good advocate for the agency's culture.

To ensure that the new hire stays engaged with the team, use these guidelines:

- Make sure that teams have regularly scheduled meetings.

- Have all team members turn on cameras to create face to face interactions

- Facilitate open dialogue where team members receive recognition for accomplishments (big and small) and share problems and concerns.

- Encourage group feedback and brainstorming to solve problems.

Ongoing Feedback

Onboarding and training are a continuous process. While we all remember how long it took us to find our sea legs when we first started in the industry, we often get stuck in a "set it and forget it" mindset regarding onboarding and training. It is also critical to remember that many of us came into the industry receiving training in a very traditional trainer-trainee set up. This arrangement kept new hires close to co-workers, providing easy access to expertise when questions arose and, very likely, more open and fluid conversation as different situations would come up around the office.

The remote environment feels different because it is different. It will require an employee to take some initiative to reach out when they need help. However, to encourage this, managers and trainers need to have regular check-ins with new hires and create an environment that welcomes questions.

Closely tied into that is the feedback conversation. In a remote environment, the ability and tendency to disconnect from the conversation is much easier. Leaders and managers must be diligent about maintaining communication and feedback. Without it, an employee can feel unsure of where they stand, if they are doing anything right, and uncertain about their job security. Scheduling feedback conversations with a new hire, however, will provide many benefits, such as:

- It helps set the tone and get the employee comfortable with these types of conversations. If they do not get feedback for six months, their guard will be up during that discussion, and it will be harder to get them comfortable with having their performance evaluated.

- It shows your investment in their success. Without feedback, an employee can feel uncertain about their relationship with you and leave them wondering if they are doing their job correctly. Regular feedback provides a new hire assurance that is especially comforting and encouraging in the early weeks and months of their job.

- It provides the employee with much-needed guidance. Continuous feedback provides managers an opportunity to point out what a new hire is doing well and address any issues before they become habits.

Performance reviews and feedback do not just need to be from the manager to the employee. Asking the employee to come prepared with feedback can provide important insight as well. Whether it is likes and dislikes about the onboarding process or challenges they encounter in the training process, this information can be beneficial as the agency continues to seek ways to improve the process for future hires.

The onboarding process presents many challenges both in-person and in a remote environment. However, as the virtual world becomes a bigger part of our reality, agencies must give careful consideration and invest time into thoughtfully planning the onboarding process for new hires. When done right, an agency and a new hire can establish a connection which helps the employee achieve their professional goals and the agency continue to grow and succeed.

CHAPTER 6:
MANAGING VIRTUAL TEAMS

"When you feel overwhelmed by all the technology and hassle of managing your remote team or project, and it seems like everything's about "process" and "over-communicating," keep something in mind. Genghis Khan ruled half the known world and never, ever, held a WebEx meeting. Not one."

— Wayne Turmel

With the sudden need to respond to the COVID-19 pandemic, many companies have been forced to adapt to the sudden need to go virtual. For companies without an existing remote-work culture, however, transitioning from a traditional office environment to a remote workspace might require significant adjustment for both the leader and the employee.

Nonetheless, running a virtual team is not much different from running an in-office team: both require strong leadership. While there are adjustments that you will want to consider in your leadership strategy, most of skills you already utilize every day will remain relevant as work becomes more and more virtual.

Establish Clear Rules and Boundaries

The idea of working remotely may be a new concept to many of your staff. They may be more accustomed to, and therefore more comfortable in, an office environment where they can see you and other teammates. Providing clarity early in the process regarding rules and expectations will help put everyone at ease. No one appreciates ambiguity, especially when everything else in life feels uncertain.

Setting rules and boundaries early on as you transition to remote work will help set you and your employees up for success. Even employees who occasionally work from home will experience a significant shift as they begin working remotely on a full-time basis, so be sure to include them in your efforts to establish clear rules and boundaries.

Be sure to address the following topics as you implement your remote-work plan.

Work Schedule

The shift to remote work inevitable raises several questions about schedules. Do hours change in a remote work environment? Should employees start earlier in the day now that they no longer have to commute? When should breaks be taken? Is your schedule as the supervisor different, and when and how can they get a hold of you if needed?

Answers should be provided on day one to avoid any confusion.

Make sure to also discuss after-hour needs. What should communication look like if issues arise outside of the regular work hours? When employees transition to a virtual environment, they become physically closer to their work, even after the workday has ended. Help your team understand that access does not create an obligation to respond outside normal work hours. Ensuring they know this is important for preventing burnout and frustration amid what may already be a stressful situation.

Workspace

Establishing guidelines for home offices is also important. Talk about what an appropriate workspace looks like. What technology do your employees need to have access to? How much privacy do they need to have in their home workspace? At the same time, not everyone's home is set up to accommodate a dedicated home office. Consequently, many employees may not have the room to separate their workspace from the rest of their living space. Be understanding of this to avoid making this transition more stressful.

Nonwork Activities

Working from home unleashes a new set of distractions to employees accustomed to an office. There's cleaning, laundry, kids, pets, and plenty other things right outside the door of their home office.

It can be easy for employees to fall prey to the I'll-just-do-this-quickly thought process, which takes the employee out of their work and into another activity not related to their job. Ensuring employees understand how those other distractions should be managed throughout the workday will help minimize misunderstandings in the future.

Communicate Quickly, Clearly, and Often

If you are accustomed to thinking "I'll talk to X when I see them," remember that this option no longer exists. Communication in a remote environment requires effort and intention. No one will be passing by your door, which means you will need to take the time to reach out to individuals.

When in doubt, err on the side of overcommunication. Sharing mundane or pointless information should be avoided, but make sure that even the smallest relevant details are communicated to everyone on the team. The level and amount of information shared should be consistent with what would have been shared when everyone was in the same office. When you endeavor to share even the fine points, you can ensure that everyone is getting more than adequate information to succeed in their jobs in any work environment.

As part of this, strive to be ultra-clear and concise when communicating with your team. You are at the mercy of technology, and it is more important than ever to make messaging direct and clear. Remember, typing a quick email is not like having a face-to-face conversation where you can quickly clear up details with questions. It can be easy to glaze over particular details when typing an email, but in a remote work environment, exchanging correspondence requires a lot more back-and-forth to get the same message across. The more clarity you provide up front, the less room there is for misunderstanding.

As a leader of the team, you must consider how you communicate now and how to enhance those skills in a remote work environment. When on phone calls or video conference meetings, make sure you are listening. Set communication guidelines, including expected and appropriate response times for emails and messages. These should be rules that everyone follows, including you as the leader. If you fail to respond promptly, individuals will start to feel the weight of separation and may begin to disengage.

Be a proactive communicator. Clarity and transparency are vital in a remote work environment because of the physical disconnect, so establish clear communication around goals, expectations, deliverables, successes, and improvements. If a strategic or business decision impacts the team, be open to sharing the reasoning for that decision so everyone understands.

Finally, be willing to ask for feedback. Your team will have questions and concerns as the business continues to move forward in a new way, so be sure to create space for them to express those feelings and suggest improvements. This kind of openness is vital to the communication health of your team.

Create Digital Interactions

When working in a digital environment, using technology to create connection and collaboration is key to employee happiness and productivity. To capture the in-person feel of team meetings, use video whenever possible, and require all team members participate on screen. While this kind of interaction can uncomfortable at first, over time the face-to-face interaction can help forge team bonds.

In addition, video conferences allow you and employees to gauge each other's reactions through facial expressions and other body-language clues. While body language is more difficult to decipher via video conferencing, you can still pick up on subtle cues that tell you whether a team member is engaged, struggling, or checking out.

Encourage frequent and impromptu communication between team members to spark the casual communication and collaboration common in a physical office. Consider utilizing interactive technology in meetings and chat group software to make this possible. And of course, make sure the entire team is informed about all communication tools available to them. The right tools will allow employees to interact more regularly and spontaneously, making them more present throughout the workday.

You will also want to make sure you are continuing to reach out to team members on an individual basis. Check in regularly, and set a schedule of one-on-ones. This will allow you connect with each person, discuss specifics of their job, and address any concerns they have in an environment separate from the group. Consider asking questions like:

- What is your workspace set up like?
- What is your daily routine?

- How do you manage distractions at home? Are you struggling with this?

- What helps you feel connected to others when you're working remote?

Taking the time to understand each team member's needs will help create a better connection between you and your team. Build on this by being intentional about sharing success stories and providing positive feedback in every meeting—including those with the whole group. Ensuring the entire group is aware individual and collective accomplishments further connects employees to each other but also to the goals and purpose of the team.

Focus on Key Performance Indicators (KPIs)

Part of strong communication in a business environment, especially a remote one, providing clarity on the indicators of success. In the transition to remote work, these indicators may have changed, and employees should be informed accordingly.

As part of this effort, discuss deliverables and tasks involved daily to keep everyone on the same page and moving in the same direction. Done consistently, this maintains a cohesive environment even when the team can't be together and clarifies how time should be spent on any given day.

Of course, there will be times when some employees fail to meet the standards laid out for them. Unfortunately, disciplinary action can be challenging to implement in a virtual work environment without jeopardizing the team member's productivity and feelings about work. Issues must be addressed carefully—you are not in the same physical space. Strive to recognize the efforts of each team member, coach them, and correct behavior that's not working.

There are bound to be bumps in the road as you and your team adjust to a new way of working and interacting. You will experience technology hiccups, deadlines may get missed, and there will be interruptions that you have zero control over. Keep calm and accept that some things won't go exactly as planned. When missteps happen, make sure you keep open lines of communication, and get everyone focusing their time and energy back on your overall goals.

Deploy Tactical Empathy

Transitions are anxiety-inducing changes, especially when the people you once depended on are no longer in the same physical space as you. Your team has no greater need than empathy during stressful times (Dan Pontefract, founder & CEO of the Pontefract Group). Empathy helps build trust and provide a feeling of stability for your team.

Recognize and be sensitive to the fact that going remote is a change in routine for everyone. Every personality on your team is going to have a different reaction to this transition. Understanding this will help you to better empathize with each of your employees.

Check in with employees regularly to see how they are adjusting. Asking questions like, How are you? and How can I help you today? give employees the space they need to express their concerns. Being an empathetic leader proves you value your team and have their best interest in mind.

Employees will be working through many different emotions during this time, just as you are. There may be days when they are edgy and challenging to deal with. Addressing those behaviors and situations may require you to dig deep and be patient. Don't react, but instead ask more questions and get clarification.

Empathy will be crucial to success for you and your team. You will want to expand this skill in any way possible and reassure employees that your primary concern is their overall well-being.

As you and your team face this significant period of adjustment, everyone will be tackling multiple things, sometimes new ones, all at once. Whether you plan to have employees working remotely on a short-term or long-term basis, it's essential to make sure you choose solutions that make sense in both scenarios. Navigating all these changes can be stressful, but implementing the right solutions will reduce that stress and help the whole team make it through this transition together.

Chapter 7:
Evaluating Emerging Insurtech

"We are stuck with technology when what we really want is just stuff that works."

— **Douglas Adams** (Author)

Since the recent emergence of insurtech, the insurance industry has experienced a rapid change in available technology. There is a wide variety of products and solutions for every part of the insurance chain with more options hitting the market every day. In this environment technology products must continuously evolve or risk becoming obsolete.

The adoption of technology is critical to the functionality of agencies, both new and old. The right technology will provide an agency, speed, reliability, and automation—all of which can provide significant cost savings and a competitive advantage at meeting increased consumer demands for rapid solutions.

However, technology alone is not a solution. In fact, it can present its own set of problems:

- There are too many options. For every product promising to solve a problem, there are at least two or three (if not ten) others providing the same guarantee.

- There is a lot of flashy, fancy technology, leading to "shiny-object syndrome."

- New technology can come with a substantial price tag that makes it simply unaffordable for an agency.

- Often a technology product includes great features but does not provide any real solution regarding time, money, speed, efficiency, customer service, or quality of work.

- New technology can also be complicated, making it challenging to use or incorporate into day-to-day operations, which presents significant roadblocks with adoption among agency personnel.

What, then, does an agency do when they know they need to upgrade? How do they find the right solution and avoid the dreaded buyer's remorse?

Identify the Problem

When beginning the process of assessing future technology investments, agencies must know the pain point they want the technology to solve. For this to happen, agencies should ask the following:

- What goals and objectives does the agency have? What is currently working that will continue moving the organization forward? What gaps still need to be filled in order to achieve those objectives in the desired timeframe?

- When the agency fell short or missed organizational targets altogether, what were the roadblocks that contributed to those issues? Is there a technology-based solution that would help the agency move around or through those problems?

- What other issues, hang-ups, or inefficiencies exist in the organization? What are the pain points associated with those issues? Can the resulting challenges be quantified? Whether they are delays in response times, missed opportunities, or customer service issues, what is the financial impact to the agency? Is there technology available that would reduce or eliminate these problems?

Technology is simply an expense unless it helps resolve a known issue or move the agency toward organizational goals. All technology must be evaluated against these things criteria.

Research

As you begin your search for technology solutions, you will quickly find that multiple competitors offer a solution for your problem. Each will promise the same solution with a few proprietary bells and whistles. Some may seem more appealing than others right out of the gate, but it is important to take the following into consideration:

- Review the cost associated with each solution, as this will vary significantly from product to product. The pricing structure may be based on overall agency size, per user, per location, per transaction, or a flat fee regardless of size or usage. Having this information to estimate the cost is a critical part of being able to evaluate the monetary investment required for the product.

- Be sure to understand how this technology connects with existing agency technology or what internal infrastructure may be needed to support it. Whether it is additional servers and storage or more internet bandwidth, there may be an additional investment required to utilize all of the product's features.

- Read product reviews. There will undoubtedly be testimonials on the company website, which will tell you part of the story. However, you will also want to do additional research. There are third-party companies that review insurance agency software solutions and publish their findings online. These websites will typically provide a more in-depth review of the features, pros and cons, and other competitors in the same space.

- Contact the company and ask for references. They should have a list of agencies available who are willing to discuss their experience with the product to prospective buyers. References are a powerful resource in the research process, as you can get a much more in-depth understanding of their experience from the evaluation phase through purchase and implementation. These agencies will be able to provide you their firsthand experience with the process.

- Learn about the size and financial stability of the company. How has the company been funded? What is the makeup of the ownership structure? This information will help you conclude the likelihood of a future acquisition by a larger company.

Organizing all these details in an Excel doc is a great way to be able to look at specific information side by side. Being able to evaluate all the information in a single view will help prepare you for the next step.

Identify the Top Contenders

As you consider the potential product offerings, a few options will need to be eliminated, and the final list should be narrowed down to three or less. Moving into the full product analysis on more than three will consume far too much time and become overwhelming very quickly.

Once the list of finalists has been determined, it is time to get an in-depth understanding of each solution through the following steps.

1. **Schedule a full product demo.** This meeting will take place between a product representative and individuals at the agency. Depending on the size and

setup of your agency, you may need to include a few team members to get a variety of perspectives.

The product demo is your opportunity to ask questions, examine all the features of the product has to offer, and start updating your list of pros and cons.

2. **List the features each product has to offer.** There will be certain aspects of each product that "wow" but may not serve a purpose for your agency—be sure not to get sucked into shiny-object syndrome. Instead, remain objective about which features are most critical to solving the problem identified at the beginning of this process.

3. **Evaluate the features of each product against the operations of each department within the agency.** It is critical to understand who is impacted by the implementation of new software and to what extent it will change the functions of each area of the company. For instance, if you are looking to bring in a product as a P&C solution, the group benefits area of the company may not see any changes. However, if you are looking at a full agency management system conversion, all departments will be impacted.

4. **Obtain all cost details.** Pricing on software solutions can vary greatly. Keep in mind that the current pricing is only one part of the picture. You will need to understand future pricing. Many software solutions may lock in pricing for twelve to twenty-four months but expect a percentage increase each following year. There are often setup fees too, depending on the complexity of implementation and training required. All these different elements can make a significant difference in the cost to the agency.

Make sure to request a proposal that outlines *all* pricing details.

As part of the cost-evaluation phase, get clear on how the product benefits the agency. Is part of the software cost offset by new efficiencies gained through implementation? Does it provide capabilities that help the agency grow faster? These details are all important factors when making a decision on which product is the right fit for the organization.

5. **Assess the overall functionality of each product.** Some products will be simple and straightforward, while others will be a bit more complicated. Understanding the ease of use of each option will provide insight into what the implementation and onboarding process might look like. Bringing in a product that is complicated and difficult to use will likely lead to an arduous training process and low adoption rate.

6. **Confirm all aspects of the training and onboarding process.** Make sure to understand how the vendor conducts training (e.g., live webinars, online tutorials, in-person trainings, or a combination of different options). It is equally important to understand what the vendor provides for ongoing support. The initial onboarding training will likely be handled by one person or a small group of trainers, but questions from employees arise as they use the product more. It is critical to understand where employees should direct those inquiries when they require assistance.

7. **Dig into the contract wording.** Most solutions are going to require the agency to sign a contract, and it is crucial to understand the nuances of each. When

dealing with contracts, you need a clear understanding of the contract duration, payment terms, cancellation fees, and opt-out options the agency may have should a larger firm acquire the company. It also critical to understand what happens with company data. Most software solutions interact with agency and client information. Knowing how the data is being transmitted and used, as well as who owns the data during each part of the process, is of utmost importance.

One other item to clarify is any pricing benefits the agency can take advantage of with a longer-term contract or larger down payment.

As with the initial research phase, outlining all these details in a document will allow you to compare the different products and quickly identify the pros and cons of each.

Make a Decision

At this point, there's been a substantial amount of time and effort invested in identifying the right product for the agency. There has likely been some back-and-forth with different vendors, and you should have *all* questions answered so you can confidently select an option and move forward with the solution that best meets the needs of the company. You have now reached the purchase and onboarding step in the process.

Once the contract is signed and the first payment is made, it is time to get to work bringing this solution into the agency. Here are the critical components of this process that will help clear a path to success:

1. **Choose a project manager**. This individual will facilitate and coordinate all different stages of the process. They will be the primary point of contact for the vendor as well as other employees. The project manager must both have an in-depth understanding of the technology and be organized, detail oriented, and effective at communication. They will work with leadership to create an onboarding strategy and communicate this information to the agency staff. It is especially critical that leaders in the organization provide support to the project manager.

2. **Schedule a kickoff call with the vendor.** The goal of this call is to map out the training plan, set an implementation timeline, and schedule future meetings to touch base. This meeting should involve the vendor trainer, agency project manager, and possibly other members of leadership to ensure everyone is on the same page. When developing a training plan, consider the number of employees requiring training. Depending on the size of the agency, you may need to divide everyone into smaller groups to ensure employees can engage throughout the session.

3. **Schedule training sessions with each group.** Although managers and supervisors need to stay informed about the process, the project manager should be the one sending invites to employees. In larger groups, it may be difficult to get to everyone without any scheduling conflicts. These issues should be brought to the attention to the project manager to ensure everyone receives the training needed, including by scheduling additional sessions as required.

4. **Establish a "go live" date.** Once trainings are nearing conclusion, the project manager should announce the date the new technology will be available to employees to use in their day-to-day work, even if workflows and process changes have already been made in anticipation of integrating this new technology. Recognize, however, that until everyone is using the technology daily, you don't know what you don't know, and discussion should be open for future modifications.

5. **Identify specific targets based on the original goals and objectives.** Leadership must create metrics to stay informed about the gains (or losses) made because of technology rollout. Using this information to evaluate progress early and often is critical. Some options for evaluation could include:

   o KPIs based on employee usage and efficiencies gained

   o Employee survey to receive feedback regarding training, onboarding, and product usability

   o Vendor feedback regarding how often and what types of requests they are receiving from employees

The information generated will provide valuable insight into the level of success achieved. Results will help the project manager and leadership understand whether the implementation plan is on track, whether modifications to processes are still needed, or whether additional training is required.

Bringing new technology into an organization is no easy task. It must be monitored and evaluated on an ongoing basis to ensure that it continues to move the agency toward the goals identified at the beginning of the process.

CHAPTER 8:
TECHNOLOGY
IMPLEMENTATION

"Risk is changing. And for me, a lot of that centers around how rapidly technology is developing and needing to be incorporated into agencies certainly, but into businesses of all types."

— Steve Anderson

Bringing new technology into an agency requires careful review and consideration. There may have been missed targets or even inefficiencies in processes that are costing the agency time, money, and opportunity. Maybe there are aggressive goals the agency wants to achieve. Regardless, the technology that is adopted should provide a solution that removes roadblocks and helps advance the overall mission of the agency.

To that end, there is a lot of research and planning that occurs before new technology becomes part of the agency's operations. This first step is critical to ensuring the agency invests in the right product.

This process will include:

- Research and evaluation of existing solutions on the market
- An in-depth review and comparison of the top three options
- Final selection and purchase
- Identifying a project manager

Once these things take place, the real work of integrating the technology into the operations begins. It is critical to recognize that this is not a one-time action, but rather an ongoing process that will require regular attention.

How do agencies implement a new piece of technology and ensure they are getting the most out of their investment?

Onboarding

Successfully introducing and implementing new technology in an agency requires a well-thought-out process and a clearly defined desired outcome. Without these both, there is not enough direction, and implementation may not successful. Taking the time to think through the entire process and develop clear goals around how this technology will improve the agency will set the project up for success.

For this to happen most effectively, the project manager must steer the project. This role will include several duties to keep all steps of the process organized, coordinated, and communicated.

- The project manager will be in continuous communication with the vendor. This person will need to develop a thorough understanding of the product. They will also need to ensure all details regarding setup, access, and training are addressed before putting the product to work in the agency.

- Many pieces of technology do not operate on their own but instead require additional servers and storage. While the project manager will likely not be the same person who sets up these additional pieces of equipment, but they will need to know who will be handling this part of the project. There is likely a timeline involved for acquiring and integrating the supporting technology. The project manager must understand these requirements and coordinate with the IT team accordingly.

- The project manager will also need to work with the vendor to understand the training options available, such as live webinars, on-demand tutorials, or an in-person or hybrid approach. This information should be used to develop the initial agency training plan.

- Most importantly, the project manager will need to develop a communication strategy, which should include general announcements to staff, training schedules, and updates to leadership throughout the process.

A solid training plan is a foundational aspect of successfully implementing new technology. Several approaches can be taken based on the type of technology being introduced and the setup of the agency, but sticking to a training plan from the beginning will help ensure a smooth adoption of new technology.

A training plan is typically coordinated and scheduled by the project manager in conjunction with the trainer from the vendor company. However, input from others within the organization will be necessary for the development of this process.

Training Plan Considerations

Is this technology applicable to every department?

The technology the agency is introducing may impact different departments within the organization in different ways. Getting perspective from staff who understand the current department setup and how the technology will change the department's day-to-day is valuable to the development of the final training plan.

Each department will need to understand the different features provided by the product and which ones will be utilized in the department. Based on that information, current workflows should be reviewed and modified to integrate the appropriate features.

Who needs training?

Depending on the size and makeup of the agency, dividing employees into smaller groups may be a great solution for successfully onboarding staff.

Groups could consist of specific departments or even roles within the agency. By using these criteria, training can focus on the features and tasks most pertinent to the work each group of employees does every day.

Keeping the number of employees in each training low will provide a better opportunity for employees to stay engaged and interact throughout the session.

What do they need to know?

Not every employee will need to know the entire system inside and out. Training should provide employees an overall understanding of the product, but the focus should be on an in-depth demonstration of the features they are expected to use daily.

Workflow training may also be necessary if changes have been made to incorporate new technology. This will help employees draw a better connection between the software and their work.

Where do they go for additional training?

Training is not a one-and-done step in the process. Whenever introducing new technology and processes, questions after the fact are inevitable and should be expected. If employees feel as though they need to figure everything out on their own, you'll notice rising frustration and a low adoption rate.

Additional training options can include recordings of prior training sessions or other on-demand webinars provided by the vendor. Make sure employees know where they should go if they need additional training. Whether an employee needs an overview of the entire system or a refresher on specific features, providing a way for them to easily access information is an essential part of the implementation process.

To help employees retain what they learn in a training, provide opportunities for independent study time so they can use the software and practice what they observed in training. The more exposure employees have immediately after training and *before* they are interacting with customer data, the better. Consider setting up a beta test wherein employees must handle scenarios that apply to how they will be using the system in the future. The vendor may even be able to help you create these extra training opportunities.

Establish a "Go Live" Date

This date is the day the new technology becomes active within the agency's day-to-day operations. Before flipping the switch, however, the project manager will want to confirm that:

- All employees have access to the new system. Ensure that all logins are operational. If there are different permission levels, confirm that the system configuration is set up appropriately and that employees can navigate to the information they need.

- All supporting technology is up and running. Getting all systems functioning can be a challenge, so testing to make sure everything is properly working is critical to a successful launch.

- Employees are clear on where to go for support. While everyone may have been through training, they will not remember 100 percent of what they learned. There are bound to be hang-ups and questions along the way. Make sure they know who to contact, when to reach out, and how to get ahold of those providing support. Whether it is a resource within the agency or assistance provided by the vendor, these guidelines must be communicated to employees so they are prepared when questions arise. This information is critical to minimizing stress and promoting ongoing success of the implementation process.

Once the project manager confirms all the above pieces are in place, it is time to put the technology to work!

When new technology goes live, it becomes an active part of the agency processes. At this point, employees should be using it as designed to manage certain tasks in their workflows.

Employees will become more familiar and comfortable with the technology the more they use it. The process changes that once felt new and different will become more fluid, but there are a couple of things to track in the early stages of implementation:

- As employees become more familiar with how the new technology and processes flow together, they may also identify steps in the workflow that do not work as well as expected. They may find better or simpler ways of doing specific processes. Ensure there is a process in place to record these findings and reevaluate the workflow for necessary modifications.

- When employees are actively using the system, they will run into obstacles and will have questions. It is important to collect these questions. Not only will this help with future conversations with the vendor as far as additional training, but documenting these questions and providing answers can become an excellent Q&A resource for other employees who may run into the same issues.

Staying on Target

Continuous review of the usage and performance of new technology is critical to ongoing success after the initial implementation phase. Far too often, agencies invest in technology and fail to follow through with evaluating its effectiveness. Whether it is in ninety days, six months, or a year, technology can often be put on a shelf and neglected by leadership. Employees will quickly abandon it as well.

To make sure your technology solution is actually a solution, don't forget why you purchased the technology in the first place.

Early in the prepurchase process, the agency should have developed a clear picture of how the functionality of the technology was going to help resolve problems or support the achievement of specific agency objectives. The goals of investing and introducing a new system into the operations of the agency should remain front and center to ensure that leadership and all employees leverage the technology.

Establishing a process for tracking specific key performance indicators (KPIs) will provide the necessary insight into how well things are working. KPIs could include:

- Employee usage
- Process time reduction

- Increased quantity of work

- Improved quality or accuracy of work

Equally important to gathering this information in the evaluation process is reviewing, learning, and adapting. Technology implementation is not static but rather an evolving process. To ensure technology continues to be effective, organizations must evaluate:

- **What is working well.** Highlight efficiencies gained and improvements the agency has made as a result of implementing new technology

- **What needs to change.** Processes and integration are not going to be perfect from day one. Remain open-minded and transparent about reviewing and modifying processes along the way.

- **Where do employees need help.** Employees may struggle at the individual or department level or with a particular workflow or product feature. Agencies must know where the struggle exists and provide additional training to rectify those problem areas.

- **Whether the technology is being used as expected.** Understanding how employees or departments should be using the technology and what is actually happening at the desk level is crucial to evaluating the adoption rate. If employees are avoiding change and relying on old processes, a system to address this resistance and hold employees accountable to expectations is a must.

- **Long-term benefits.** Your new technology needs to offer benefits in the long run for the effort put into implementation to be worth it. Pay close attention to:

- The continued evolution of the product

- Whether the technology is still driving desired results and adding value to the organization

- Whether the ongoing cost is still reasonable and sustainable

- Additional solutions that become available in the market

Technology upgrades of any kind can be a sizeable investment for an agency. To successfully implement new technology, leadership must be committed to tracking progress and addressing snags in the process of any kind. Doing this will ensure that organization continues to leverage technology to generate growth and opportunity for the agency.

PART 2:
THE 50 MOST COMMON QUESTIONS ASKED BY INSURANCE PROFESSIONALS

1. What Should You Do When Your Top Producer Is Driving Account Managers Out?

I have a small commercial lines agency with four producers and five account managers. My top producer is also my biggest problem. While he brings in a lot of quality business, his demanding behavior and lack of attention to detail has been a nightmare for our account manager. Over the past two years, I have had to replace three account managers who have all pointed to him as their reason for leaving. He is not crude, and he doesn't yell. But he is unrelenting in his efforts to get his own way, and it's killing office morale. How do I motivate him to change before another account manager quits? I don't want to lose him as a producer, but I can't afford to keep replacing account managers.

Your agency has a high-performing producer bringing in quality business and meeting new business goals year after year. The problem is, there is a revolving door of account managers because of this producer's behavior. This situation is a tough but not uncommon dilemma many agencies face.

What should an agency do when they encounter this very problem? Here are a few things you will want to consider when deciding on the next steps.

- Evaluate the producer's behavior against what the agency considers reasonable and prudent conduct between staff. Does the behavior meet those guidelines? Ignoring this type of behavior can have a long-term effect on the rest of the agency. While turnover may be the most pressing concern, allowing this type of behavior sends a message to other employees within the agency that leadership is condoning it. Left unaddressed, it will quickly erode agency culture.

- Have an open and honest conversation with the producer who is causing the problems.
  While you might assume that the producer is already aware of the issue, they might be oblivious to how their behavior is impacting other people or the organization. The conversation should happen sooner rather than later and focus on the specific behaviors contributing to the resignation of other staff. This discussion should be an opportunity to discuss the problem and appropriate solutions. These solutions should be actionable by the producer and measurable by the supervisor. Ensure there is a process in place to follow up and monitor progress.

- Review alternative setups to alleviate stress. Perhaps the friction is stemming from being in the same office. If this is the case, moving the producer to another location or a home-based setup will provide enough distance between the agent and the account manager to reduce tensions.

- Recognize that while this is not strictly a dollar and cents issue, the resulting turnover is costing the agency time and money. It can take weeks, if not months, to find and hire a new employee. There is also a time and cost component to onboarding and training a new employee.

It can be very challenging to deal with a producer who brings in revenue but simultaneously damages relationships within the agency. Chances are your agency will encounter this issue more than once, and it is critical to be prepared to handle the situation the next time it arises.

As you continue to weigh the options, keep in mind these reasons from Gary Vaynerchuk for why you might need to fire your most talented employee:

- Toxic employees will slow your organization down. Employees aren't spending time executing if they're thinking about who's trying to "ruin" them.

- We are at the dawn of an era where emotional intelligence will be far more important than technical skills.

- The speed of your company is determined by your internal culture.

2. How Do You Deliver Bad News to a Client?

I have been in my role as an account manager at our agency for the past five years. Our owner recently shifted accounts around, and one that I received is renewing shortly and facing a substantial rate increase. It does not look like the prior account manager prepared the client for this increase nor did they look for other competing options. How do I deliver bad news to the client without having him take it out on me?

Situations will arise that require an employee to have a difficult conversation with a client. Having this conversation can feel incredibly stressful, especially if the situation is not the result of the agent's actions

For example, an account manager is handed new accounts due to the department's shifting of work. Upon reviewing their new file, the manager notices a substantial premium increase on an account that is just about to renew. Although they were not responsible for everything that happened with that renewal leading up to now, they are responsible for communicating with the client.

This situation is certainly not an ideal sequence of events, but here are some things to consider if you are in that situation.

- Review the file with the prior account manager. They may know why the renewal submission did not get sent to other carriers, and they can clarify how much discussion (if any) has taken place with the client regarding the rate increase at renewal.

- Discuss the rate issue with the producer. Depending on what communication looked like with the prior account manager, the producer may not be aware of the rate increase their client is about to be hit with at renewal. The producer may have some thoughts on the best way to present this information to the client, or they may want to handle that conversation themself.

- Reach out to carriers to find out if there is any way they will accommodate a last-minute request to quote the renewal. Provide full details regarding the rate ahead of time. This way, they can make an informed decision as to whether they will be able to provide a competitive quote.

- Communicate with the client sooner rather than later. It is better to provide as much advanced notice as possible rather than catching the client off guard when an invoice arrives. Be direct and apologize for the situation. Provide clear information about the challenges with the renewal rate and the steps you are taking to find an alternative solution.

- To prevent this type of situation in the future, make sure you have a robust process in place to review renewals well in advance of their expiration. Implement a marketing plan that is reviewed by every producer for every renewal. Proper planning will help keep all parties involved on the same page.

These types of conversations are certainly not easy to have. However, taking ownership of the problem, communicating, and seeking solutions will help you continue to build valuable problem-solving and conflict resolution skills.

3. How Do Small Agencies Compete in an Aggressive Job Market?

My agency is small yet profitable, and we have a solid team in place. That said, I'm finding that my newer hires are expecting salary increases beyond what the agency can afford to pay. How do I keep talented people when I don't have the funds to compete with the big brokers, and how do I communicate to my account managers that there's only so much I can afford to pay for their specific role?

Attracting and maintaining talent in insurance agencies has been a growing challenge in the industry over the last few years. Smaller agencies may feel they are at a disadvantage against larger brokers when it comes to salaries and career growth opportunities.

What options does an agency owner have when employees are seeking something beyond what the organization can provide?

Have an open conversation with employees about their expectations regarding salary and career.

This conversation will allow them to express their concerns with their current wage and the changes they think would be appropriate. This discussion is also an excellent chance for you to find out their long-term career goals.

Be transparent about advancement opportunities that exist within the agency.

- If an employee's desired income and career path are beyond what you can offer, they must understand upfront what the limitations are. Embrace the opportunity to help them develop in their career and achieve their professional goals even if it means they ultimately outgrow the company.

While it may seem counterintuitive, being a good leader for this employee may mean helping them find their next role with another organization.

- Suggest alternative solutions. While the agency may not be able to offer more money for the position, perhaps other benefits would appeal to the employee like additional time off, more flexible scheduling, or an option to work from home. You may find that these are all options that help offset many employees' salary concerns.

- Ensure employees are aware of the value of the small agency environment you are committed to maintaining. Even if you cannot compete dollar-for-dollar when it comes to compensation, employees need to understand the value you do provide.

  As a smaller operation, you're able to offer certain perks, whether it's a commitment to a forty-hour work week, an emphasis on family time, or flexibility, that aren't subject to burdensome management layers. These perks may not be immediately obvious to employees who have not had enough experience to know how other agencies operate.

- Implement a robust training plan. There are no guarantees of how long an employee will remain with your agency. By creating and implementing a strong training plan, you will be in a better position to handle those staffing changes as they arise.

The insurance market will remain competitive from a talent acquisition and retention standpoint. Taking the above steps sends a strong message of honesty and transparency, which is critical to building and maintaining an agency culture attractive to employees.

4. What Skills Does an Account Manager Need to Handle Difficult Customers?

I've been working as a junior account manager for several years. I am more of an introvert by nature, and I also don't like conflict. I'm struggling to deal with customers when they get angry on the phone. I become flustered easily, which makes it even worse. Sometimes I feel like snapping back, but I know that will get me into more trouble. How do I stop a client from bulldozing me while still being empathetic?

When working in a customer service role in an insurance agency (or any industry), there is bound to be conflict. It can certainly be frustrating if your goal is to help the customer, and they do not respond positively to your efforts.

Here are some strategies for handling those challenging client conversations:

Be Empathetic

Empathy is the ability to understand and share the feelings of another. Finding empathy can seem almost impossible depending on how angry a customer may be on the other end of the phone. Try stepping into their shoes for a moment to reevaluate the situation and get to the root of the issue. Chances are, there is an underlying issue to their level of frustration.

They may have had a bad experience with the service provided by the agency in the past. Or perhaps they are having a rough morning with a temperamental toddler. Either way, taking a moment to dig into what is going on will allow you to find out what you can do to help.

Slow Down the Conversation

As a client tries to communicate information while stressed or angry, there is a good chance they may speak louder, faster, and nonstop. The combination of these things can certainly create more communication barriers. As a tactic, you can very calmly and respectfully interrupt the conversation. Let them know your top priority is to help, but you need to record the information they are providing accurately. Politely request that they slow down so you can be sure you don't miss any critical details. Framing the request as part of your desire to help will provide needed reassurance of a common goal.

Choose Your Words and Your Tone Wisely

Just as the client's tone and choice of words can have an impact on you, the same goes for the words and tone you choose in response. You can try explaining to them what you are sensing with a simple statement like, "It seems like you are very frustrated." Another option is to repeat back to them what you hear with a response along the lines of, "It sounds like you're frustrated because we didn't get that information for you when you needed it." The client may confirm or correct your statement. Either way, you have conveyed to the client that they are heard and understood.

Clarifying to the client what you are hearing or sensing can be powerful because it lets the client know you share their concerns and allows the client to reflect on how they are communicating.

Reach Out to a Supervisor

If the options above do not work to diffuse the conversation, and the client continues to yell or be otherwise disrespectful, it is time to get someone with more authority. Politely excuse yourself from the conversation by saying something like, "This is no longer a productive conversation. I am going to put you on hold while I get a supervisor who can help us work through this problem." Allowing someone else to assist or take over the conversation may be the best route to finding a resolution to the problem at hand.

Most customer interactions will be pleasant and positive, but there will undoubtedly be those that seem impossible to win. Implementing these tips will help you better manage those stressful conversations, leading to a better experience for both you and the client.

5. What Should You Do When a New Employee Is Disrupting Agency Culture?

I recently hired an account manager away from a competitor of mine because of his expertise in our niche, but it's been a rocky start. He keeps refusing to follow our processes and makes a point of bringing up how the other agency used to do things. It's starting to rub my staff the wrong way. How do I get this guy to fall in line without creating an enormous amount of conflict so early in his employment?

Finding a talented individual for your agency who also brings valuable insurance experience to the organization can feel like a huge win, especially in a competitive job market. As exciting as this is, it is crucial to recognize that this employee's past work experience means they are likely accustomed to a different way of doing things under their prior employer. This experience can become an issue if the new employee disregards the guidelines and processes that are in place at your agency and refuses to embrace a new way of doing things.

So, how can agencies avoid this type of conflict altogether? And what should an agency do if a new employee is dragging baggage from an old job into their new one?

- Identify culture fit during the interview stage. If possible, bring in other team members during the interview process. This open interview not only allows the candidate to meet the rest of the group, but it will also allow you to observe how they interact.

You will be able to better gauge how well the potential new hire will adapt to your agency's culture. If something seems off in that interviews, that is a strong indication that this candidate will not be a good long-term fit for the organization.

- Utilize a robust onboarding process. When bringing a new employee into the agency, it is critical to provide as much clarity as possible. Make sure your agency has well-documented processes and procedures for how employees should handle each task of their day. Proper onboarding lets employees know what systems the agency has in place to review and evaluate current workflows so that they have a full understanding of when they should supply feedback.

Suppose you are in a situation where you have already brought an employee into the organization and find yourself facing challenges with their performance and lack of cooperation. In that case, you will need to take the following critical steps to remedy this issue:

- Have a conversation with this employee. Provide open and honest feedback about the importance of following the processes and procedures as outlined and how it impacts their performance. Communicate clear expectations about what needs to change and improve. Clearly state what the consequences are if these changes do not happen. Within that same discussion, take some time to remind them about the existing agency policy on how and when they should provide input to existing workflows. This conversation is also an opportunity to explain how their behavior is impacting others in the organization.

- Monitor employee activity and look for improvements in performance. If the issues do not resolve, this is a clear indication that they are not the right fit for your agency. Once their unfitness becomes evident, it is critical to cut ties and allow that employee to move on to their next great opportunity.

It can certainly be challenging to address employees' performance issues, especially when they are new to the agency. However, waiting for problems to correct themselves only prolongs the situation and will harm the entire organization. Using the steps above will allow you to create a plan to take action when it is most critical.

6. How Do Agencies Provide a Flexible Schedule to Employees?

I've been at my agency for nearly ten years now as an account manager, and I'm really struggling with a double standard that exists for producers versus account managers. I have missed my kids' ballgames and school events because our agency doesn't allow time off to account managers unless we use vacation time. Meanwhile, even new producers are allowed to come and go as they please. And one of them in particular has a son playing baseball in the same league as my son. Last Tuesday, our two teams played against each other. He attended the game, and I couldn't. I don't know how common this is, but it seems as if some employees' family commitments are much more important than others, even when they've been with the company for far less time. How would you suggest I handle this? And what would convince you as an agency owner to change this office policy?

The traditional workweek in an insurance agency is quickly becoming a thing of the past. No longer is the nine-to-five, Monday-through-Friday office hours the norm or the expectation. Employees are looking for companies that provide a family-friendly culture and offer more choices as they strive to meet the demands at work and home. Whether it is doctor's appointments, kid's events, or other commitments, employees are looking for ways to make it all fit into the week.

So how do agencies meet the increasing employee expectation for flexibility and continue servicing clients?

- **Rotate flex time.** Examine your team's overall setup and ask employees to provide feedback regarding when they would need to be out of the office to fulfill other obligations. Once you've put this information together, work with the team to create a rotation where they provide backup support to one another throughout the week. By creating a schedule, you can ensure that system is equitable to all involved.

- **Provide on-the-go access.** Most phone and email systems provide a way to forward calls and emails to a mobile device. This option will allow account managers to handle urgent issues with clients that may come up when they are away from the office.

- **Set clear expectations.** Ensure employees have a clear understanding of their responsibilities when it comes to making flexible scheduling a success. Everything from expectations around making up flex hours to how calls and emails are forwarded to their cell phone should be handled and clearly communicated to your team. This information will keep everyone on the same page.

- **Document the flex scheduling policy.** Documenting agency guidelines will ensure all employees have the clarification they need when it comes to opting for a more flexible schedule. This policy should address the specific aspects of your agency's flex schedules, such as maximum hours permitted, when and how to make up flex hours, and usage of mobile devices for agency business.

- **Start with a trial run.** Providing a flexible schedule option to the entire organization could get overwhelming and challenging to manage quickly. By starting with one department or a smaller group of employees, you can assess what is working with the system and make necessary modifications. Once you've worked out all the glitches, you can open the opportunity to other employees.

- **Evaluate success.** As implementation continues to grow across the agency, leaders must keep tabs on how things are working. Make sure to check in with employees for feedback. The chances are that the flexible scheduling policy's original guidelines will need to be reviewed and modified as time goes on. Establishing regular checkpoints will ensure that the program continues to evolve to meet the needs of your employees, clients, and the agency overall.

The demand for a more flexible workweek will continue to rise with current staff and new employees. Recognizing and having a plan to meet this need will help your employees achieve the work and home lifestyle they desire.

7. How Can Agencies Create a Training Process that Sets New Employees Up for Success?

I run what some would call a small or midsized agency. My problem is that my staff is less than excited to help our new hires. Everyone says they're too busy and looks at me with blank stares when I ask for help. Most of them had someone to show them the ropes, and yet they seem to be uninterested, unless there is something in it for them. They don't seem to process that it is in their best interest to get the person up and running to share the workload. How do you get your staff to contribute to the training process in a way that gives the new team member the best chance of success?

Helping new employees get off on the right foot when they come to your agency is not only critical to their long-term success, it also contributes to how likely they will remain with the organization. Training is vital to ensure those early days for a new employee go as smoothly as possible.

What should agencies do to create a training plan that sets new employees up to succeed sooner?

Make It a Team Effort

Placing all the responsibility for training an employee on one person is very likely not going to be an option that generates the right results for the trainer or trainee. Not only does it place a considerable time constraint on one employee, but it could also create training burnout for one employee.

The advantages to deploying a "divide and conquer" method are:

- Every employee has different strengths. When an employee trains a new team member in the area where they are the most comfortable and proficient, the new employee will benefit from the trainer's expertise.

- Allowing a new employee to learn from different staff members provides an opportunity to get to know and build relationships with all team members.

Agencies can segment training between the agency management system, carrier systems, department workflows, other agency processes, or in any other format that makes the most sense to the specifics of the organization's role and operations.

Develop a Process and Procedure Manual

Every agency needs a guidebook that everyone can reference. While some more seasoned employees may have steps of the process memorized, it is critical to have documented procedures. New employees will need a process handbook that they can easily reference, especially after working more independently.

Go Digital

Gone are the days of heavy procedure manuals that require employees to read through pages and pages to find an answer. There is a good chance that new employees coming into the agency are accustomed to digital learning as they have been consuming video their entire lives.

Invest in a decent microphone and software, like Zoom, and have your team record procedures on video. While this may seem a little uncomfortable for your team, there are significant benefits, including:

- Digital resources are accessible for new employees to reference on their own whenever they need to, so they will interrupt other team members less.

- Documenting processes with video provides a new employee consistent information.

- Video workflows can be easily updated as processes change.

Taking the time to create a digital workflow resource will save everyone time and support consistency.

Training new employees can be time consuming and frustrating for everyone involved. These three steps will help ensure your agency can significantly reduce the friction in the process and set new employees up for success in their role.

8. How Do Agency Owners Integrate Outsourcing into Their Agency Operations?

We are thinking about using an outsourcing company to reduce the back-office processes for our account managers. The hope is that we will be able to take a lot of work off the account managers' desks and allow them to work on higher priority items. However, I am concerned that this may leave my account managers without enough work to fill their days. How can we add outsourcing services and make sure everyone stays busy?

Outsourcing has become an increasingly popular option at agencies across the country to handle the data entry and back-end processes that do not require client interaction. Agencies have found this to be a great way to fill entry-level positions as the pool of eligible candidates continues to shrink.

It also frees account managers to focus on more high-skilled, relationship-building tasks for clients. While this arrangement does present a significant upside, agency leaders must be able to understand how this solution can work for their organization.

Here are a few useful tips for agencies as they integrate outsourcing practices into the agency's operations.

- Make sure you have a full understanding of responsibilities that are eligible for outsourcing. Have account managers provide a list of all processes that do not require client interaction. Ask them how often they perform these processes each day and approximately how much time each one takes. This information should provide clarification on the actual need for outsourcing. It will also give you the details you need to calculate the number of hours per week you could save current staff by transferring tasks to an outsourced employee.

- Help your team understand why this change is necessary. As work shifts over to the outsourcing company, some staff might have concerns. Whether it is a fear of losing their job or concern about general expectations, it is essential to provide answers to any questions they may have on the subject. Taking the time to discuss and explain the long-term goals of integrating outsourcing will reassure employees with the details they need to understand how this benefits them in their role. Discuss details about how outsourcing will allow account managers more time to dedicate to the functions that are most critical to building client relationships.

- Talk to your team about how this change may include new services to clients that they did not previously have time to handle, which ultimately allows them to develop new skills. Ensure individuals understand how putting all of these pieces together will allow them to focus on value-driven tasks that ultimately influence retention. Maintaining open communication about why and how everything will work together will help employees get on board and buy-in to a new way of doing business.

- Ensure employees have clarification regarding the separation of duties. Workflows should be updated to note any tasks that should be handled by the outsourcing company. Providing these specifications to Account Managers should help reduce any confusion around who should be handling what and lower the likelihood that anything falls through the cracks.

- Establish guidelines for accountability. Integrating outsourcing is an ongoing process that will require continuous management to generate the desired results for the agency. You will need to identify any shifts to the process needed along the way. The right KPI's will demonstrate the level of effectiveness outsourcing is having on the agency, whether it leads to increased retention, reduced overtime for in-office staff, or increased output for the company overall. It is, therefore, critical that leadership maintain oversight and review of KPI's regularly.

Outsourcing can be a significant change and present unique challenges. Putting these steps together will help agencies prepare and implement outsourcing practices into the operations.

9. What Should Agents Do before Signing a Producer Agreement?

I am about to change positions within my agency from service to sales. I'm very excited about this next stage in my career, but I have heard nightmare stories from other agents about not getting paid fairly and being charged agency fees and expenses. I'd really like to make this career change work, but this feedback from others is a little concerning. Is there anything I should be aware of before I make the leap?

The insurance industry is no stranger to contracts. From carrier contracts to insuring agreements, contracts dictate a lot of what happens within an agency. Even agents are required to sign a producer agreement before they go to work for an agency. The purpose of the agreement is to outline specific terms of employment. But like any contract, there can be a lot of details that are difficult to decipher.

As eager as an agent may be to get to work, it is vital to do a few things before signing on the dotted line.

- **Have the contract reviewed by an attorney**. A producer agreement can be full of legal terminologies. Some parts of the contract may be straightforward, but other sections may have more complexity.

    An attorney will be able to review all the fine print and advise you on any details that raise red flags or create complications down the road. An attorney will also understand state statutes and identify any illegal or unenforceable conditions in the state where you work. Investing in legal advice to ensure that you understand all aspects of your contract before you sign will save you stress in the long run.

- **Be prepared to negotiate.** Whether or not your attorney has advised specific changes to the contract, you and your employer may need to amend the agreement. Understand that you have the right to review, discuss, and ask for changes to the terms of the contract before you sign. Once you sign, this becomes a lot more challenging. Embrace the opportunity to negotiate the points in the agreement that are most important to you.

- **Don't be afraid to ask questions.** Entering into a contract with an insurance agency is an exciting step. However, it is perfectly reasonable to have questions and concerns. Whether you need more information about licensing, training, or compensation, getting answers upfront is better than putting the pieces together after the fact. Obtaining as much clarification as possible will help prevent future stress and help move all parties toward future success.

- **Understand how the agency plans to invest in your future.** If your goal is to build a career in the insurance industry, you must work with an agency committed to helping you meet those goals. Look for key indicators of the company's commitment to your growth, such as investments in your continued learning and development and a well-designed marketing plan that provides you the exposure you need as you begin a career in sales.

A career in insurance is exciting and rewarding. By taking a little extra time and paying attention to the details before signing an agreement, you can be sure you are as prepared as possible to start your career on the right foot.

10. What's a Good Quote-to-Bind Ratio?

I am a producer, and the principal at my agency has been on my case lately about my quote-to-bind ratio. I'm frustrated because I am hitting all of my new business goals and quoting fewer accounts for the sake of a quote-to-bind ratio will likely mean less new business for me. I understand that she's getting pressure from our insurance carriers, but wouldn't they rather have an agency submitting more business than less? What's a good quote-to-bind ratio that will keep my agency principal off my back without negatively impacting my new business?

Insurance producers go to work each day seeking opportunities to make sales. Not only is there a financial benefit to the producer, but they typically will also have a sales goal they are trying to reach. However, the pressure to meet a sales goal can often cause producers to pursue a lot of prospecting without generating profitable results. This meaningless activity can create more work (and frustration) for everyone involved. Additionally, this work costs agencies time, energy, and money.

Here are a few steps every producer should take to refine their sales process.

- **Understand the rules of engagement.** When working with a new client, it is essential to understand how *they* want to work. Neither party wants to get to the end of the process and find out that both sides' expectations didn't match up. To avoid this type of frustration, producers need to ask questions that provide opportunities for the insured to clearly express what the agent needs to do to earn their business. Agents should get details upfront regarding their client's premium threshold, expected timeframe to receive quotes, or service level requirements. This information allows the agent to decide if they can deliver on those expectations before investing time and energy into the process.

- **Be upfront with underwriters**. Upgrades in carrier technology have provided greater capabilities for agencies to handle quoting from the comfort of their own offices. However, there is still a significant amount of business that needs to be submitted to the underwriter to review and quote. To maintain a competitive advantage, agents often take the liberty of sending a submission to every carrier regardless of whether the specific carrier can secure the business. This practice can substantially waste the underwriter's time and eventually damage the working relationship between the agent and the carrier. To prevent this resentment, agents need to be transparent with their intentions. Whether a submission is sent only to block a market or the agent knows which premium would make the carrier a viable option, having an open dialogue from the beginning makes the process easier for all parties involved. Clarity and transparency will help maintain productive relationships between agencies and carriers.

- **Openly communicate with your sales manager.** While an agent's sales goal will probably not change throughout the year, understanding what it will take to meet those goals can feel like a moving target. It can be hard to gauge when there's too much prospecting and quoting and not enough closed sales. Seeking clarity from your sales manager about what they define as a healthy quote-to-bind ratio is a meaningful conversation. These discussions can also be an excellent opportunity to review achievements, evaluate strategies, and examine parts of the process that need to continue moving toward more success.

- **Accept that you can't win them all, at least not right away.** Even if an agent follows every step of the process to precision, they cannot expect to successfully close every sale. There are many reasons why a prospect still won't sign. They may have a relationship with their incumbent agent that is difficult to break, there could be a more competitive option available, or it is merely going to take more time to build trust and confidence with that prospect. Whatever the case may be, making an objective assessment will allow an agent to learn from their experience and decide how to change their approach in the future.

There is no cookie-cutter, one-size-fits-all method when it comes to selling insurance. However, implementing the items above will help agents get on the right path to developing an effective sales process.

11. How Do I Make the Transition from Account Manager to Producer?

I've been thinking about becoming a producer, but I'm not completely confident that I am cut out for a role in sales. I'm also not sure if the opportunity will be available at my current agency. I'm in this industry for the long haul. What is the best way for me to start making my way into a sales role in my agency?

Building a sales career in the insurance industry can be extremely lucrative with the potential to make an excellent living. And while the producer role is not right for everyone, if you have the desire and the grit to take a run at a sales position, the payoff can be very rewarding. A role in production often affords flexibility, the opportunity to determine your earning potential, and residual income on retained accounts.

If you have been in a service role for a while and you're interested in trying your hand in sales, here are four critical items to understand about making that transition.

Test Drive Your Sales Skills

While a sales role can be advantageous, there are also a lot of risks involved. If you are not 100 percent confident that you are ready to leave the safety of a salaried service role, there are ways to test out the sales water before taking the plunge. One great way to do this is by upselling and cross-selling with clients in the book you are currently servicing. Helping them understand the value of additional insurance options that provide better coverage is a critical part of the insurance sales role.

Executing this with clients you are familiar with can help you better understand your future sales role potential.

The personality traits that it takes to make a great service person are different from those required of a successful salesperson. Confirming that you have the right traits for sales ahead of time can be a great way to make sure you do not get in over your head.

Develop a Business Plan

Knowing you have a desire to build a career in sales and having the knack for it is only part of the battle. Having a plan to build your accounts book is an entirely different but critical part of a successful transition in sales.

Explore options with various types of businesses that pique your interest. Once you have narrowed it down to a few niches, start investigating how many prospects exist within that niche and estimate your potential income based on earning a percentage of that business. Evaluating different niches and their earning potentials will help you laser in on the right path when you do step into a sales role.

Discuss the Opportunity with Your Supervisor

Understanding and then verbalizing goals can be a little bit intimidating, but it is crucial to your ongoing development. Your supervisor won't assume that you are interested in moving into a sales role. Demonstrate your willingness to share goals with your manager to display your tremendous amount of initiative. If you can, validate your request for a new position by showcasing the cross-selling you've done with your existing service book and the sales plan you've developed. Revealing that you already have those skills will go a long way in landing the pitch with your manager.

The conversation with your manager is also an essential step in understanding the opportunity that exists within the agency, what a sales role would look like, whether part-time or full time and expectations that are part of that role. All of these points are necessary to make sure both you and your manager are on the same page where you want to go and if the agency you're at can get you there. And if they can, identify the next steps to make that happen.

Be Prepared to Move On

There is a harsh reality that your current agency may not be able to facilitate your request to move into a sales position. The agency may not have an open position for sales. They may not have enough support staff to absorb your work, which would include your current service book and future producer book. Or they may not feel you are the right fit for a sales role.

Regardless of the reason, you will have to decide whether you stick with your current agency with the hope that an opportunity will eventually open up or move onto another agency where you can transition into your desired role.

12. How Do You Handle Hygiene Issues in the Office?

I'm a male agency owner, and it has recently been brought to my attention that there are some hygiene issues with one of my employees. It's become frequent enough that other employees complain about her. She seems very unaware of this problem, and I'm concerned about saying something that will get me sued. Have you ever dealt with a situation like this before? If so, how did you handle it.

There is a logical expectation that your agency employees will follow appropriate hygiene and sanitary practices. Your agency very likely has a section in the employee handbook that covers general guidelines about personal hygiene. It is typically a safe assumption that employees will follow it without much discussion required. Unfortunately, this does not always happen as it should and, if left unaddressed, can become a bigger problem for your employees and clients who need to work with the offending individual.

Once an employee brings a coworker's hygiene to your attention, it is essential to act before the stink becomes a problematic stench (literally or figuratively) that interferes with work and performance. While approaching an issue like employee hygiene can be uncomfortable, here are tips you can use to have a helpful and productive conversation on a very awkward topic.

Get Necessary Details

Obtaining relevant details is critical to ensuring that the issue presented warrants a response from a supervisor. For example, what is causing the odor? Offensive odor from overuse of perfume or cologne will require a different approach than body odor resulting from a lack of proper hygiene. It's also essential to understand how long the issue has been going on to determine if this is the result of a new behavior. Both of these things are important for understanding the full scope of the problem.

If it sounds like this is a new development, it might be wise to wait the situation out for at least a few more days to see if it improves or remedies itself. However, if it is apparent that the issue has been present for a while, it is essential for the well-being of all employees that a conversation addressing the problem takes place sooner rather than later.

Recognize Other Contributing Factors

The chances are that the employee did not just develop this problem overnight for no reason. Finding out if the employee in question has mentioned any major life events to colleagues is vital. These things can impact and disrupt an employee's regular habits, even when it concerns personal hygiene.

If an employee has a new love interest in their lives, they may feel compelled to go a little heavier on the perfume or cologne. More importantly, however, understand that a lack of personal hygiene and self-care can be a sign of depression and anxiety. If an employee is becoming withdrawn or easily frustrated on top of neglecting good hygiene, there certainly could be a personal crisis that requires even more careful and compassionate handling.

Handle the Conversation Delicately

Whether the odor is caused by an overuse of perfume or poor hygiene, it is understandably difficult to tell an employee that the way they smell is offensive to others. There is no easy way to get that message across, and it is reasonable for an employee to feel defensive. Utilizing both professionalism and empathy when delivering the message is critical.

Keep the conversation as private as possible. If necessary, have another manager or HR representative present to discuss the issue. Use the employee handbook and review the agency policy on hygiene with the employee. Once you have had a chance to address concerns, make sure to have an open discussion about workable solutions.

While a conversation on a topic like odor and personal hygiene can be uncomfortable, it's essential to address it in a way that respects all employees' rights. Using the tips above will help you facilitate a conversation kindly and work toward a solution from which everyone can benefit.

13. How Do Agencies and Producers Execute Effective Marketing Plans?

The agency I work for provides a higher commission split overall for producers but does not reimburse for any of our marketing expenses. Recently, I was approached by a recruiter for a large regional agency, and while the splits are not as high, they're offering to provide a lot more marketing support than I'm currently getting. I would like to get my agency to provide me with a marketing budget. What advice would you have to best negotiate that with my current agency?

Brand awareness is a critical component of both insurance agencies' and their agents' success. Access to the right marketing can be the difference between reaching your target audience and missing the mark altogether. For marketing to be effective, agencies need to dedicate resources like time, money, and effort.

A marketing plan that lacks design and planning will fall flat with little generation of sales. To create a workable plan, agencies must critically understand that marketing represents them and their agents. Let's look at a few essential questions to get you started on developing a marketing plan.

What Is the Ideal Audience, and Where Do They Hang out?

Selecting and understanding your audience is vital to your plan. Without this information, the only option is to start throwing different marketing at the wall to see what sticks. You'll quickly discover that it's impossible to track what is working and why. Replicating the most effective parts, therefore, becomes nearly impossible. The "try everything" approach is ineffective. Expenses can start to add up very quickly despite a lack of direction or clarity gained from your marketing efforts. There is, therefore, no way to narrow down your strategy and get your expenditures under control.

Instead, focus your efforts. Decide on your target client. If it's personal lines, start narrowing prospects down to a specific demographic. If working on business accounts, start looking at specific classes or types of businesses, an ideal premium size, and other characteristics that help create a meaningful marketing plan for that type of client's specific needs.

What Cost Is Involved, and What Is the Desired Return?

As noted previously, marketing can be costly. Even items that seem minor can come with a hefty price tag. Without parameters, marketing can quickly start to eat into your agency's budget. Agencies must be focused and intentional with marketing expenses.

Start by understanding who you want to reach and where to find them to reduce wasted marketing efforts, be it time or money. During the client research phase, it is essential to figure out the best way to reach your prospects. If most of your audience is located outside of your community, taking out billboard ads will not generate much activity. It would be much better to invest in a digital strategy. Knowing how and where you can get your audience's attention is critical to ensuring you get the most bang for your buck.

A marketing plan also needs to include the expected return to understand its level of success. The expected return could be an estimated number of leads and the desired percentage of closed sales. Failing to define these parameters will leave an agency guessing what is useful and what is not. Taking time to specify anticipated outcome means agencies have a marker for measuring results. It also means agencies can identify what methods are working, where adjustments are needed, and any marketing efforts generating little to no return. Once this happens, campaigns can be even more focused, further reducing wasted time and money invested.

How Much Is the Agency or the Agent Willing to Invest? How Should Expenses Be Handled?

Knowing how expensive marketing can be, there must be budgetary guidelines set by the agency. Unmonitored marketing will start to eat at company resources very quickly. Consequently, agencies must decide what makes sense when it comes to their budget. Agencies can allocate budgets in several different ways, but anyone, including producers, who relies on marketing to grow the business must know the structure.

Providing support for a marketing campaign is essential, but there should be controls. Producers do not necessarily know what will or will not be effective. Guidance from an individual with marketing expertise paired with an expense limit is necessary. An agent joining associations, attending meetings, or taking out digital and paper ads can all be considered part of marketing. Setting a budget will help keep the producer in check and protect the agency's bottom line. If a producer feels the budget is too low to fit their needs, consider negotiating this with a reduced commission or allow them to invest their own money. When producers add their own money to the pot, they have an increased interest in seeing their investment pay off. It provides flexibility in the budget and allows the agency to maintain necessary control, which protects the interest of the agency and the agent.

Marketing is an essential element of agency growth. Developing a marketing plan with appropriate guidelines can help agencies and their agents work together to identify and achieve common goals.

14. Is There a Right or Wrong Agency Dress Code?

The dress code for the agency has changed over the years and is increasingly becoming more casual. The problem is that I think our producers need to dress more formally, especially when meeting prospects and clients. I'm experiencing a lot of resistance as some serve different types of customers and the dress standards are not the same. How would you handle this in your office?

It does not seem that long ago that the typical insurance agency office was full of men in suits and ties and women in skirts, blouses, and nylons. There has been a substantial shift over the last three decades to a much more casual approach. That shift continues with employees pushing for an even more casual and laid-back dress code.

There is no right or wrong way to write a dress code, but here are few things to consider when modernizing your company policy on acceptable attire.

Prioritize Culture over Tradition

The truth is that attire in most business sectors has relaxed considerably. Each generation that enters the workforce is a little (or a lot) more casual than the preceding one, and it is apparent in every aspect of their lifestyle. This desire for a more casual way of doing things shows up in their expectations for work. As tech startups encourage a much more laid-back office setting, this mindset has found its way into the insurance industry. While suits, ties, dresses, and heels are traditional, they're not necessarily attractive to the insurance workforce's future members.

Creating a culture that offers flexibility when it comes to everyday wardrobe choices will make the agency more attractive to new talent. It provides room for employees to assert their personal style. It's also an opportunity to show the agency focuses more on developing good employees than on who irons their khakis every morning. Focusing on the person as opposed to the wardrobe will help agencies identify critical factors when it comes to whether an individual can do the job.

Some Occasions May Call for Different Attire

Not all work situation demands the same outfit. If an agent is going to visit a client who operates a quarry, a suit is not necessarily going to be the appropriate dress for the occasion. Some clients may be uncomfortable with certain types of dress. Going to a dirty job site in a three-piece suit might intimidate your client, whereas a polo shirt and jeans could put them at ease and make you more relatable to the client. However, a meeting with the president of a large bank may have different expectations. Understanding and adapting to the situation with appropriate wardrobe choices is essential to connect with clients.

If you choose a more laid-back look for typical days in the office but need employees to dress up for specific events or visitors, it's essential to make sure those expectations are clear to all staff.

Develop a Written Policy

Providing flexibility without creating a free-for-all is critical. Therefore, strive for a written policy that strikes that balance. With the proper guidelines in place, employers can have a policy that does not require micromanaging. It can also call on employees to utilize good judgment and common sense when choosing work attire.

Well-designed dress policies will hit major dos and don'ts of acceptability while still giving employees flexibility and freedom to choose what is comfortable, acceptable, and feels good. A policy can be vague while still providing clear ground rules that allow HR and supervisors to address problems and provide guidance for employees if they question something.

While there are undoubtedly many traditions worth keeping, an outdated dress code may not be one of them. Using the information above will help you evaluate what the right fit for your agency is.

15. A Producer Is Leaving and Wants Me to Come. What Should I Do?

I am an account manager at a large agency. The producer I worked with for years has been unhappy with the agency for quite a while now for several different reasons. He is now telling me that he plans to leave, take his clients, and even asked that I go with him. I feel like he's put me in a tough position with the agency, and I don't know what to do. What is my responsibility in this situation?

The day-to-day operations of an agency can be full of complications of varying degrees. Often, the complexities arise from interpersonal relationships or difficult workplace situations. Both can cause internal and external conflict. It can seem at times that there is no right answer, and even finding the right next step can feel like a losing battle. When employees encounter these difficulties, there is a tendency to ignore them and move on. While avoiding problems feels like the more comfortable option in the moment, the tension can build up and cause more significant issues in the future. Instead, evaluate the situation and work through it.

When faced with difficult situations at work, it can be stressful and hard to decide what to do next. Here are tips for tackling those dilemmas:

Get the Facts

It is human nature to make assumptions and jump to conclusions. It is the path of least resistance. The brain wants a solution now, and creating one based on limited information is easier than the alternative. Operating under assumptions can cause us to do things and create more problems down the road. Doing this means we solve the case without relevant details.

For instance, picture yourself as an account manager at an agency. The producer you work with comes to you and tells you he plans to leave for a competing agency and plans to take his book with him. You may feel shocked and overwhelmed by this information.

It is easy to see why this message is concerning, and you instantly want to try to figure out what to do with this new information. In this situation, it's crucial to slow things down and make sure you have a full understanding. Get to the root of the situation with the following step:

1. Ask the producer if he has discussed his decision to leave with the agency principal. Is he working through the necessary process to make the transition smooth for him and those clients that wish to stay with him? If he hasn't, encourage him to do so. If he refuses, then it may mean you need to take additional action.

2. While you are questioning what your obligation is in this situation, consult the agency employee handbook and see if there are any answers. If the handbook does not provide answers, consider talking to the HR department. An HR professional should be a safe person for you to express your concerns confidently without fear of consequences. They should also be able to provide clarity regarding your responsibility in the situation and provide appropriate guidance for the next step.

Don't dangerously assume that the agent is planning just to sneak out and has not done his due diligence. Such an assumption can easily damage your relationship with the departing agent. And if he hasn't done what he should, acting without a clear understanding of what you're required to do can make the situation even more stressful.

Take a Step Back

When facing an uncomfortable situation, like the one above, it can be hard to be objective. When it feels personal, it is critical to hit the pause button on the thoughts, solutions, and conclusions running through your head. Take a step back and question why you are wrestling with this situation. What is it that is causing the conflict? It might stem from one of the following:

- If the agent has not told ownership and is not obligated to do so, are you questioning his ethics?

- Are you concerned about the security of your job if he leaves and takes the book with him?

- Are you now feeling the weight of responsibility for someone else's decision?

There could be several specifics about the position you find yourself in that feel uncomfortable and bothersome. Slowing down and stepping back can help you identify where you are struggling.

Discuss with Someone Outside the Situation

Even after obtaining additional information and stepping back from the situation, it can still feel like you're too close to the problem. Finding someone you can trust and talk to that is completely detached from the situation can prove beneficial. This person could be a spouse, significant other, parent, friend, or colleague in the industry who does not work for the same agency.

Ideally, this person knows you and your personality. They will provide an outsider's perspective, which will help you find the clarity you need. Consulting with someone like this can help you understand where your struggles stem from and provide options you can use to deal with the problem.

Dilemmas are a natural part of our personal and professional existence. Using these tips can help you gain the perspective and clarity you need to find your way to a solution.

16. What Kind of Challenges Are There When Returning to Insurance after a Few Years in Another Industry?

I've been working in the insurance business for the past five years. Recently an opportunity outside the industry came up that I'm interested in exploring. However, I'm fearful that if I want to return to working in insurance, I'll have to start over at the beginning. What are your thoughts on this? How difficult do you think it will be to get back in?

For many years, insurance agencies have been able to thrive with minimal turnover. Employees would begin a position at an insurance agency and build a career, often remaining in the same position for the entire duration of their career. Employment at an insurance agency provides stability, flexibility, and growth opportunities that appeals enough to most employees to keep them in the industry once they arrive.

However, a lifelong career in one industry might not be the right fit for everyone. Some agents may desire a change of pace. Here are some things to consider if you are looking to take a hiatus from insurance.

The Door Back into Insurance Usually Remains Unlocked

Leaving on good terms is critical to ensuring there is a way back should you decide you want to reenter the insurance sector in the future. As long as you've built a good reputation based on hard work and dedication and can exit without burning any bridges, returning to insurance should not be all that difficult. The industry continues to look for talent, and those with any level of experience remain highly sought out.

However, it is essential to keep a couple of things in mind if you want to return after a few years:

- Retaining your license will be critical. You'll need to take ownership of your continuing education and any necessary filings required to keep your license active. Being able to apply as a licensed insurance agent will help put your resume at the top of the stack.

- Do what you can to stay current on changes in the industry. Whether you leave for two years or five years, there will be changes. Keeping a finger on the pulse will help you be better equipped to dive back in if the time comes.

- There will be a learning curve. Even if you retain your license and keep up on continuing education, technology will change. Being prepared to learn and adapt when you join an agency is critical to your success.

Other Experiences May Prove Beneficial

You can learn and grow substantially from exposure to other industries. No one industry has all the answers to its specific business problems. Putting an insurance career on pause may be an excellent opportunity to gain valuable work experience in something that is not directly related to insurance but is very applicable.

Acquiring new skills, Exposure to new processes, and interactions with people of various work backgrounds can powerfully boost your professional growth and learning.

Putting those pieces together and applying them to your insurance career can be a significant advantage when you return.

There Is More Than One Path to a Successful Career in Insurance

When you decide to return to the industry, it may look different. The same position you previously worked in may not be available.

The agency may want you to take a couple of steps back to ensure your skills are up to par with the requirements of a job. And while these may seem like setbacks, they can also be a calling to look at other opportunities.

While some may find it rewarding to return to the same position after a few years away, it is certainly not the only option. The insurance industry offers a wide variety of career paths. You may quickly discover when returning to insurance that you can be in an industry that you love and pursue other roles within the industry that interest you.

Stepping away from the industry for a few years may be intimidating, but rest assured, the opportunities will remain. Taking the time to plan for a return before you exit can help solidify your future career options when you choose to rejoin the insurance industry.

17. How Do I Set My Son or Daughter up for Success in the Family Agency?

I want my son to come into the business, but I think it would be best for him to work at another agency for a couple years to get some good experience and build credibility before coming into our agency. What are your thoughts on this?

For many years, the insurance industry has thrived with independent agencies building a legacy by passing their operations from one generation to the next. And while the industry has seen a lot of consolidation activity over the last few years, there are still thousands of second- and third-generation independent agencies run by the original owners' children and grandchildren.

To keep the tradition alive, agency owners must have a plan to usher in the next generation. There are a few critical items you'll want to keep in mind as you prepare to bring your child into the agency.

Provide the Right Training

While it may be tempting to have your son or daughter get some experience outside of the family agency, this can create complications. It will be challenging to find an agency that wants to invest in an employee they know will leave to run their family operations. If they find a job in another agency, they will start their career investing time and building a book for someone else only to leave it behind when they join the family agency. It also means they are learning from and building habits that might not mix into the family agency's culture and operations, which could lead to conflict down the road.

Instead of passing off those valuable formative years of your son or daughter's career, remember that you have all the people and tools you need to train them right within your agency. Additionally, this means you can share your experiences and lessons as an owner (both good and bad). You also control which employees will provide additional training. Your child will get the opportunity to learn about insurance from you and the people you trust the most within your agency. They will also develop a full understanding of the ins and outs of running the agency so they can carry on the business with the same level of integrity with which you built it.

Communicate with the Agency

When bringing a son or daughter into your agency, transparency is critical. If the plan is for your son or daughter to take over operations in the future, attempting to cover up or minimize it can create animosity amongst other staff. Also, assuming that all employees understand your plans with the agency is dangerous territory. While many kids of owners grow up in the agency, visit frequently, and maybe even have odd jobs around the office from time to time, this does not automatically communicate to staff that your son or daughter is their future boss. Until you formally hire your son or daughter, plans for who will run the agency remain ambiguous.

To avoid or reduce bitterness when your child does come into the agency, make sure that you communicate with the rest of the team. Let them know what your child will be doing within the agency and share what you can regarding plans.

Manage Expectations

Once you and your child decide it is time for them to start working in the agency, you may find yourself filled with high hopes about the future. After all, you have dreamed of passing the business on to them to continue the family legacy. It is an exciting time.

However, certain realities need to be kept in mind. For example, your son or daughter may not be the right fit for the industry. If they are working in production, you may find out they do not have strong sales skills. If they arrive with a sense of entitlement and do not adapt to agency culture, this will be problematic. Being prepared to have tough conversations and provide coaching where needed will be critical to their future with the agency. And if it turns out the agency is just not the right place for them to build a career, it may become necessary to let them move on to another opportunity. Setting clear expectations will be critical to their success and to your parent-child relationship at the same time.

The chance to bring your son or daughter into a business you love is an incredible opportunity. Using the steps above, you can put together a plan that creates a prosperous future for the agency for generations to come.

18. What Do Leaders and Employees Need to Understand Regarding Agency Financials?

Our agency owner doesn't share financials with us, and I think it's to avoid discussions about raises or bonuses. What is your position on this, and what is your agency policy on sharing financials?

Insurance agency financials play an important part in painting the overall picture of an organization's health and performance. This information is reviewed and used by agency owners and leaders to make strategic decisions for the company. And while this information is most critical to owners and leaders, employees can naturally be curious about the agency's stability and success.

Some agencies may keep most or all financial information locked down while others are willing to share specific details more freely. And while there may be a desire for complete transparency when it comes to agency financials, there are critical points leaders and employees must keep in mind when discussing this type of information.

There Is No Requirement for Agency Owners to Disclose Financial Information

While there may be a general curiosity among some employees to have access to financial information, this does not create an obligation for ownership to disclose details. The only information an owner must provide to an employee is that individual's wage, sales, and lost business data for those in a production role. Anything outside of that is really up to leadership's discretion to decide what is appropriate for staff and what is discussed only with those making financial decisions.

The depth of financial information agency leaders choose to share with the rest of the company will vary from organization to organization. It could be as straightforward as sales and retention or more detailed like overall revenue, profit, and contingencies.

Financials Are Complex

Financial information for any company can be full of complicated information and cause more confusion. This confusion can occur when an employee sees a profit and loss statement for the first time. Very rarely is this information black and white. One financial statement may show specific figures, but not account for other factors that impact the bottom line.

Both leaders and employees need to understand that there are complexities when looking at the agency's financial information. Most of it is not easily digestible, especially to those who lack experience looking at financial reports. Not taking the time to simplify and explain financial information to employees can create a misunderstanding that leaves employees with more questions than answers.

Address Specific Concerns Individually

It's natural for employees to be interested in the financial health of their agency. Employees want to know that the company is stable and that jobs are secure. When agency leaders are willing to share high-level financial information about the organization, it can provide the reassurance most employees are seeking.

However, some individuals may have specific concerns. Ignoring those concerns can create distrust with the employee and cause the employee to seek answers or sympathy from coworkers. It is best to provide that specific employee the opportunity to share questions so you can address their uneasiness. Taking time when addressing the individual's needs to minimize their stress and prevent their fears from spreading to other employees.

There is no one right answer when it comes to sharing financial information agency with employees. Using the information above will help leaders find clarity and prepare for those conversations.

19. How Can Agency Leaders Understand and Correct Gender Wage Disparity?

I am currently managing a department in a large agency. I was recently reviewing salaries for my employees and noticed a large wage disparity between a male and a female employee. They have the same role and equal levels of experience. The male employee is paid significantly more. I've been given a little flexibility with adjusting the female employee's salary, but there's still a gap. I don't feel comfortable signing off on their salary levels, but I don't know that I have a choice.

The business world's awareness regarding the wage gap between men and women has grown increasingly over the last few years, and the insurance industry is certainly no exception. Despite the increased attention to this problem, progress towards a solution has been slow. Some agencies may still shy away from acknowledging or discussing the issue, but that does not make it any less real or meaningful.

The severity will vary from agency to agency, but here are some tips to understanding where disparity issues may lie in your agency.

Remain Open-Minded

While the gender wage gap is undoubtedly more personal for women than men, it can be a hot button issue regardless of your sex. If you experience a lot of strong emotions when this issue comes up, you must be able to take a step back and neutralize those feelings. While a certain amount of passion is good fuel to persist through the problem and find a solution, too much can cause you to overlook important details or turn leadership off from the discussion altogether.

Instead, take time to understand how you are reacting and why. Avoid jumping to conclusions or making assumptions as this will only generate unnecessary stress. Acknowledge the information that you find and use your energy to start formulating solutions.

Research

As noted above, jumping to conclusions based on limited information can lead to more problems. When you discover or receive questions regarding a wage disparity issue in your agency, take time to do some research. Data is critical when it comes to understanding the full scope of a problem and generating workable solutions.

As you do your research, look at various roles and corresponding job descriptions, salary ranges, employees' gender in those roles, and pertinent work history. Each of these factors is important in understanding the calculation of salaries for agency employees.

Address the Problem

When the question of wage disparity arises at your agency, it is essential to take action. Doing the appropriate research, as mentioned above, is a critical part of the process to ensure you have a complete understanding of how serious the problem may be within your agency. However, once you've had time to assess the scope of the issue and can confirm that there is some level of unfair payment practices in the agency, you must be willing to take steps to correct the problem.

Solutions may include adjusting salaries of underpaid individuals and modifying hiring practices to make sure that salaries offered to future employees are consistent with the range of the role being filled.

Wage disparity will continue to be an important topic of discussion in the insurance industry. Taking time to understand your agency's role in making the industry better as a whole for all genders will help move progress faster.

20. What Does a New Employee Need to Know about Navigating Agency Life?

I was recently notified of some unethical behavior at my agency. An account manager confided in me that the agent she works with has asked her to complete his online continuing education courses because he does not have time to handle it himself. What advice do you have for someone in this situation?

Early in your insurance career it can be challenging to understand all the ins and outs of how an agency operates. The thought of saying no and standing up for yourself in problematic situations may feel a like an intimidating prospect, but not every request deserves a yes. In fact, automatically agreeing to everything asked of you can have unintended consequences. When you find yourself usure of how to respond to a coworker's request, follow these steps.

Listen to Your Gut

Early on in your role, it is normal to feel like you don't have a good sense of what is an acceptable request and what is not. The confidence you need to separate those two is not yet developed. However, when a request comes to you that sounds questionable, your body will generate a physiological response of some sort. While some of this can be attributed to nerves of being in unfamiliar territory, it is wise to listen to that instinct and at least allow yourself to question the validity of the request.

It may be something as simple as a request that is outside the normal workflow to something more serious and even unethical. Either way, slowing down and listening to your gut rather than automatically saying yes can save you some heartache in the long run.

Defer to a Supervisor

When a questionable request comes across your desk that makes you feel unsure about what to do next, do not make assumptions about how to handle it. Whether it is from a coworker or client, attempting to guess your way to a solution can end in frustration and the wrong course of action.

Instead, reach out to a supervisor. Explain the situation and allow them to guide you through the appropriate next steps. While you may be attempted to handle the situation on your own, reaching out for clarification and direction shows maturity and a willingness to learn. It also gives you an opportunity to learn that right way to handle the situation the first time around, meaning you're equipped to respond whenever a similar request comes around again.

Lean on a Mentor

You will need a trusted advisor at every stage of your career, but the mentor relationship is especially important in the beginning. As you begin your career, you will have so many questions and feel unsure of your capabilities on a daily basis. Much of what you need to know will be oriented to coverage and process. And while a mentor will help provide knowledge specific to the job, they will also be able to provide insight of their own experience. A mentor is a valuable resource for handling a difficult conversation and can also be a sounding board as you continue to navigate new and unfamiliar territory.

A good mentor will listen and provide advice without judgment. When a request comes in that feels questionable in your gut, your mentor can help talk through the problem and work with you to find a solution.

Getting to a point where you can rely on your own instincts will take time. Using the tips above will help you utilize the right resources and build self-confidence to better handle difficult situations.

21. How Do I Regroup Our Agency Leadership Team and Conduct More Effective Meetings?

The agency I work for has a large leadership group. We meet monthly to review the status of each department, overall agency strategy, and any other items that need to be discussed. Unfortunately, meetings tend to lead to disagreements or general digressions taking the group off course. Our meetings often go over without the agenda being touched. How do I regroup this team so we can make decisions that help move the organization forward?

One of the many responsibilities of being an agency leader is attending meetings. Meetings scheduled with clients, other leaders in the organization, individual employees or teams, or carrier reps can quickly fill up calendars. And while there is value in pulling people in the agency together to review, regroup, and strategize on agency initiatives, meeting fatigue is real. And even though virtual meetings reduce the time it takes to "run" from one to the next, it can still be exhausting and rob individuals of productivity.

Here are some tips for reducing meeting overload and Zoom burnout.

Prepare for the Meeting

Proper preparation is key to the success of any meeting. Failing to plan before the meeting can lead to wasted time once you gather everyone together. When preparing, remember these critical items:

- Decide who needs to be at the meeting. This tip may seem obvious, but depending on the purpose and cadence of the meeting, not every scheduled time will work for everyone. Understanding who is required to achieve meeting objectives best and who is optional will help guide decisions around scheduling and rescheduling.

- Set an agenda for the meeting in advance. Ask participants for items they want on the list and set a deadline for submitting them to the organizer. If the agenda is left open-ended, participants may feel they have room to add items and request adjustments to a finalized meeting schedule. Also, if any documents are pertinent to the agenda, collect and distribute those ahead of time so that all attendees have access and can adequately prepare for discussions.

Assign a Meeting Leader

Every meeting needs someone to take charge. Without someone leading a meeting, the conversation can quickly get off topic. Discussions that are more appropriate for another time and place can consume the entire meeting. Once this starts, it is hard to get a meeting back on track and address the meeting's goals. This can make many of the meeting attendees tired and frustrated with the time they have just invested without any results.

The meeting leader does not necessarily need to be the meeting organizer. However, it should be someone familiar with the agenda and goals of the meeting. It is a challenging role depending on how long-winded or unfocused participants are. It will require someone with tough skin who is willing to stick to the schedule, cut people off when they run over their allotted time, and shut down unproductive discussions. As difficult as it may be, this role is critical to ensure that the meeting continues moving forward, and those meeting objectives remain a top priority.

End on Time

We have all felt the frustration of a meeting that goes on past the scheduled time. When an end time is perceived as fluid by one or more persons involved, it can lead to more off-topic discussion and side-barring throughout the meeting. When a meeting runs long, it can create a domino effect of scheduling conflicts throughout the day. This lack of structure leaves attendees feeling rushed to fulfill their other obligations.

Committing to and honoring an end time shows participants that you respect their time. Also, knowing that there is a defined end time for the meeting can help keep the agenda on track.

Meetings are a part of doing business with others and can have a positive impact when done well. Using the tips above can help your agency improve and conduct more effective meetings.

22. How Do I Bring Employees Together after a Rocky Acquisition?

The agency I work for has grown steadily over the years organically and by acquisition. A recent purchase brought six new employees. After that, it became apparent that the owner regretted his decision, and his employees were also not happy with new ownership. We are being left to integrate a team that really doesn't want to be here and its harming our agency's culture and productivity. What can I do to get these team members to buy into our vision and positively contribute to our culture?

Any acquisition presents a variety of complications from a business and cultural standpoint. Often, employees are left unaware of what is happening behind the scenes until the purchase is final. This type of announcement typically comes as an unwelcome surprise. Tension can result as both agencies struggle to figure out how they will adapt and work together in the future.

As challenging as this process can be, here are tips agencies can use to bring another agency into their operations.

Speak to Individuals

During an acquisition, owners and managers should expect some level of concern from employees of both agencies. Whether employees are being acquired or worrying about the details of absorbing a whole agency into their organization, there is likely to be some stress and anxiety.

However, concerns are rarely unanimous. Some employees may not have any worries at all. Those who are having a hard time adjusting may share some common anxieties, but the struggles will be unique to the individual. Sitting down with each person one-on-one is the best way to identify and talk through their struggles and hesitations. Whether it's work hours, salary, coworkers, or agency culture, addressing those concerns an individual basis will help create a safe space for the employee to share their feelings and find solutions.

Schedule Team-Building Activities

In most acquisitions, all (or most) employees from one agency join another. This often requires two groups of strangers to start working together in a concise time frame. Employees accustomed to a specific culture, a particular way of doing things, and a team they have been working with suddenly need to merge worlds. This transition can be unsettling even from the outside looking in. Culture, process, and communication difficulties can plague the process and make it difficult for two teams to start operating as a single organization.

While some components of the merger will take time to overcome, bringing teams together in fun and safe ways can be a great way to break the ice between them. Survey each team member for ideas on activities everyone can do outside of work. These are great opportunities for them to get to know one another and establish common ground in a neutral, low-pressure situation. Once they are relaxed, they are more likely to start building a foundation for healthy relationships they can transfer over to work.

Analyze the Process and Adjust

No acquisition will ever go perfectly from start to finish, and each will have its own unique set of hurdles to overcome. However, agencies can always improve the process.

When acquisitions occur, leadership must be willing to take a step back and look at it from start to finish. Evaluate what went well and what needs to change for the next time. Soliciting feedback from those involved and impacted is an essential part of understanding each facet of the process so you can make necessary adjustments for the next time. Creating a checklist that can be reviewed and modified for future reference can help keep everyone involved on the same page.

Merging two agencies can be challenging from all perspectives of the agency operation. Using these tips will help agencies improve and reduce bumps in the road each time.

23. How Should I Deal with an Unpredictably Moody Coworker?

I am an agent in a small office with seven employees. One of the account managers has demonstrated some significant mood swings and snaps at people. It has gotten to the point where people avoid her. I know she has some difficult things going on in her life, but I don't think it's fair that everyone else is left walking on eggshells. I've reported her behavior to her manager, but nothing changes. Is there anything else I should be doing to improve this situation?

As nice as it would be for our personal and professional lives to remain separate, the two often intersect and impact one another. If appropriate boundaries are honored, then the impact of personal matters creeping into our professional lives will be limited. However, as work and home merge closer and closer together, it can be difficult to draw those lines. When it starts to affect the rest of the staff for a prolonged period of time, it will be detrimental to the agency and the work that everyone needs to do.

When employees struggle, here are some methods you can use to help overcome those challenges.

Go Directly to the Employee—Be Honest but Empathetic.

When a coworker is irritable and short-tempered, it can quickly impact everyone who needs to work with them. And while the easiest path may seem to be ignoring the behavior and hoping it goes away on its own, chances are the behavior will continue and possibly worsen.

Rather than gently walking on thin ice around your irritable colleague indefinitely, an honest approach is best. Make some notes about how the behavior is impacting you and your work. Remember, there is no need to represent the whole group. In fact, this often causes the individual to feel like everyone is against them. Instead, use personal statements, like "I feel" or "This is what I'm seeing." Calmly express your thoughts and feelings in an understanding and straightforward way. But you must also ensure that your tone communicates that you are not angry, but rather coming to them with the goal of helping them find a solution.

Be Willing to Risk the Relationship

When a coworker starts to exhibit irritable behavior that is out of the ordinary, there is a good chance that there is a bigger issue at play. It could be work related or it could be something problematic in their personal life. Regardless, it is likely a sensitive subject.

Being direct while still deploying empathy is critical to creating a safe space for the employee to share their problems without exasperating an already stressful situation. Depending on the severity of the problem, your coworker may need significant help and may not be able to appreciate your outreach in the heat of the situation. Recognize that while you may want to preserve the relationship you have with the individual, an intervention that puts a friendship or working relationship at risk may be necessary.

Identify Appropriate Support

Depending on what is causing the sudden increase of stress for the employee, there will likely be immediate and more long-term needs.

Taking time within reason to understand the scope of the problem and what support looks like in the short-term and in the future is important. Some of what the employee needs may be provided by the agency. This could include things like assistance getting professional help, adjustment of their workload, more regular check-ins from coworkers or a supervisor, or even a leave of absence. Support can look like many things. Enlisting the help of those whom the employee feels comfortable confiding in and making support a team effort may be the best way to get a friend and colleague through a very difficult situation.

Stress levels of employees will have peaks and valleys with personal triggers for each person. Using the steps above will help you navigate and support those difficult situations.

24. How Do I Make Effective Use of Time Spent with Carriers?

As the most recently hired employee at the agency, I am the lowest member of the totem pole. I have now been tasked with meeting carriers who are not high on our priority list. Instead of telling them we're not going to grow, I am forced to meet with them and make empty promises. I don't feel like this is the best use of my time, and it is a little uncomfortable to meet with them repeatedly to save face for the agency. Is there a better way to handle this that is fair to everyone involved?

When it comes to making the most of each day of work in an insurance agency, time management is essential. The issue of time is especially applicable to the constant barrage of meeting invites that chime in our inboxes daily. Meetings can quickly consume hours of our days and cause a significant blow to productivity. While meetings occur with different parties for different reasons, the carrier marketing representative meetings can be particularly challenging. Depending on the number of markets the agency works with, these meetings can multiply and add up very quickly.

These meetings should help both the agency and the carrier meet specific business objectives but require time and attention. Here are tips for managing your carrier meetings.

Take the Honest Approach

While some meetings will take place with marketing reps from your top carrier, there will also be those that need to happen with markets you haven't had so much success with.

When meeting with your top markets, it can be gratifying to sit down, look at the numbers, and applaud the success you're having. Meeting with others will not be quite as fun.

When meeting with some of your low priority carriers, you want to be honest. There is no point in spending time making up reasons why the submission rate is not so great or how it will be better in the future. Instead, look at it as an opportunity to have a candid conversation about the struggles the agency is encountering. Be honest about those struggles, whether it is their appetite, a lack of the right accounts in the market, coverage forms, or pricing. Let them know in a very open and straightforward manner what the agency would need to find success in the future. This directness will help steer the conversation toward real solutions so the marketing representative can accurately assess what they need to deliver on going forward.

Limit the Time Involved

Some carriers will want to meet monthly or quarterly, and some you may see once a year or less. And while it may seem like you should accommodate all these requests, there are only so many hours and a lot of other work to be done.

When scheduling these meetings, recognize that you do not have to agree to an hour just because a rep asked for it. Depending on the frequency, an hour every month or every quarter may not be the best use of anyone's time since agency production or any carrier needs might not change much in such a short time frame. Scheduling meeting frequency that makes sense to the amount of discussion that needs to be covered will help everyone make the best use of the time together. Using an agenda will keep meetings on schedule and better organized.

Don't Burn Bridges

As noted earlier, time is valuable. You can't get more time, and the thought of giving an hour up to a low priority carrier can feel completely unnecessary. However, these meetings are part of the agency-carrier relationship.

Blowing off a meeting or refusing to entertain business conversations can be detrimental, even if the carrier is not a critical market at that moment. Insurance is a large industry, but small and very connected at the same time. Burning a bridge with a carrier can quickly become a regrettable mistake. Carriers adjust their appetites and underwriting guidelines. Sometimes they come out with rates and coverage that are unbeatable. Rather than make a decision that leaves the agency out in the cold, do what you can to preserve an amicable relationship and leave the door open for potential future success.

Effectively managing time and carrier relationships can certainly be a challenge and often present a bit of a conflict. Using these tips, you can find a way to do both!

25. How Do I Recoup an Earned Bonus When Agency Leadership Is Refusing to Pay Up?

I started a new job as a sales manager at an agency and secured a bonus during the salary negotiation process. I have now been told there will be no bonuses. I've met the goals, so how do I get the bonus I've earned without straining my relationship with upper management?

Bonuses are commonly used across insurance agencies to incentivize and reward growth. And while calculation and payment are typically straightforward, there can be issues in any area of the bonus agreement that are ambiguous. This lack of clarity can lead to issues when it comes time for the employee to collect.

While problems with bonuses are rare, here are some tips to help you reduce your room for error.

Review the Contract

Anyone who has been in insurance for any amount of time would agree, we live in a world of contracts. Whether it is the policies we're selling or those dealing with our employment at the agency, contracts play a critical role in our lives. Therefore, just as insurance professionals review insurance policies for errors and ambiguities, you should closely review your employee contract. Assuming that everything discussed and verbally agreed upon is present in the contract can leave you at a loss.

Instead, take time to read through the contract. Confirm specific goals, time frames, and bonus amounts match what you had noted from negotiations. Also, make sure to look for any unique conditions that would allow the agency to reduce or eliminate the bonus. For example, suppose a condition requires agency growth of a certain percentage for anyone in the agency to be eligible for a bonus. In that case, your bonus is now contingent on your department and the success of the entire organization. Awareness of these details before you sign will justify you going back to the table for revisions if needed.

Appeal to Management Respectfully

When something goes awry with a bonus, it can cause a variety of emotional responses. However, if you're new to the agency, you may feel pressure just to let it go and hope it resolves itself in the future. Keep in mind, approaching upper management in the heat of the moment will typically leave you more frustrated and potentially in hot water with agency leaders. But letting it go can demonstrate a lack of confidence.

Instead, make sure you have all the necessary data and have correctly calculated the bonus you've earned. Present all the details to management along with the verbiage from your contract. While they should already have this information, taking time to assemble it can help them focus on the issue you've uncovered. If they still decline to pay a bonus at this point, requesting an explanation or plan for future payment is well within reason.

Get an Attorney Involved

While no one wants to take legal action against their agency, it may become necessary. If you cannot make any headway with leadership regarding bonus agreement language and the appropriate data to support payment, reinforcement may be necessary.

An attorney will be able to review and confirm your understanding of the contract. They can also help guide you through the next steps with the agency. While this may create tension in your relationship with leadership, an attorney can often resolve the issue quietly and get you your bonus.

Tackling a breach of contract issue with your agency can be complicated and uncomfortable territory. Using the tips above, you can more easily navigate the situation to a resolution that works for everyone involved.

26. How Do I Deal with Declining Quality and Productivity from a Former Top Performer?

I manage a small team and one of my employees is struggling with her productivity and quality of work. She usually is very on top of things, so this is out of the ordinary. We've talked about some improvement objectives, but work has continued to decline. It's time for a more serious conversation, but it seems like she always has an emergency issue with a client. Any thoughts on how I should handle this situation?

It is always difficult to watch a top performer in your agency start to demonstrate a decline in performance. There can be a tendency to bend over backward to overlook the growing performance issue and save the employee in hopes that they will turn things around. However, turning a blind eye is damaging to the employee who has the problem and other employees in the agency who are observing the situation and potentially picking up their coworker's slack.

Ignoring the problem prolongs the situation. Instead, use these tips to address the issue and help both the agency and employee move forward in the best way possible.

Identify the Underlying Issues

Getting the whole story may be uncomfortable for some depending on your relationship with the employee. However, it is essential to realize that most employees don't wake up one day and make a conscious decision that they are going to stop giving their best effort at work. There is typically an underlying issue that is negatively affecting the employee's performance.

Approach the conversation sensitively and with empathy, and make sure you're able to explain where you are noticing performance issues. Ask if there is an issue impacting their work and give them space to explain without judgment. The employee may be reluctant to share, and they may be very transparent. In either case, you must respect their right to privacy and confidentiality. If an employee feels their privacy is at risk, they will be less trusting of you and less likely to open up about the problems impacting their work.

Outline an Improvement Plan

Once you have provided the employee an opportunity to share where struggles are stemming from, you'll also want to provide them specific feedback of where their performance is suffering. Share adequate details regarding tasks or processes where quality is declining. This information will allow the employee to fully understand where work is declining and assess how to approach the problem.

While it may feel more comfortable to hand the employee a solution, this really should be a collaborative effort. Take time to discuss what steps are needed to improve the work and a timeline for resolving the problems. This collaboration allows the employee to take ownership of the problems.

Schedule Regular Follow-Ups

It is nice to think that once a discussion has happened and a plan is in place the rest of the process will take care of itself. Unfortunately, this is not the case. Getting an employee back on track is not a once-and-done process. You will need to put in additional effort to make sure improvement is stable and consistent.

As part of the improvement process, make sure you have scheduled check-points. This follow-up could be things like running reports to verify work is improving or checking in for progress via phone or email. Documenting these check-ins keeps everyone accountable for the agreed process and eliminates surprises down the road.

Know When It's Time to Move On

While it would be great if all performance improvement discussions and planning played out according to design, there is a chance that the employee will not follow through. It can be challenging to let an employee go who is struggling, but sometimes it is necessary for the employee's good and the rest of the agency.

When it comes to releasing an employee from their job, it's essential to approach the situation with compassion. Even if performance has continued to decline, it is healthier for all to be empathetic to their struggles and treat them as though they were doing the best they could.

Addressing performance problems with a struggling employee is never easy, but it is necessary to help the employee and agency move forward in a better direction. Using these tips, you can approach and manage tough conversations with more ease and fluidity.

27. What Options Do Employees Have to Update an Old and Tired Office Environment?

The office I work in is old and tired. It's sadly reminiscent of Milton's basement office in Office Space. Some might find it to be borderline depressing. The aged wallpaper, low ceilings, and poor lighting are starting to wear on everyone. I've tried convincing management that the office needs a facelift, but we can't even get a fresh coat of paint. How do I convince management to make some much-needed improvements? And is there anything I can do to lift the mood short of buying everyone red staplers?

Some insurance agencies boast modern buildings with sleek exteriors and fresh interiors. On the other hand, there are still many agencies on the opposite end of the spectrum. They operate in old buildings that meet the minimum required maintenance but leave even simple updates at the bottom of the to-do list. While some agency owners see the appearance of the building as a necessary investment for creating an inviting ambiance, it's not a priority across the board. And while the wrong environment can send the wrong message to both employees and clients, it can present a challenge when an owner doesn't see the problem the employees are staring at every day.

Here are a few tips you can use if your office needs a makeover without breaking the bank.

Appeal to Management

You may have been down this road before without positive results, but it is always worth another try to see if you can make some headway on the matter. Depending on how your agency is structured, you may be bending the ear of a manager or the owner. Regardless, it will help if you have an ally to build your case for the much-needed improvements.

When you have the conversation, come prepared with specifics. Have photos of the most glaring problem areas in the office, feedback from other employees about how the less than appealing work environment is affecting them, and even a budget for tools, materials, and labor needed for the updates. The more information you can provide, the better chance you have to make your case and get the green light for the updates. Even if you only get a few things on the list approved, recognize that as a win and a step in the right direction.

Make It a Grass Roots Effort

If pleading your case with management doesn't work, there is still room for making improvements to the space. Making it a team effort can be a great way to build morale and get a few of the updates you are looking for at the same time.

A grassroots effort could take shape in a couple of different ways. Perhaps management approves a limited budget, which allows you to buy materials but requires employees to donate their own time to do the work. And if management will not fund any of the projects, it may require employees to pitch in their dollars for paint and brushes. Either way, make it a fun, collaborative event where everyone works together for a common cause. Order pizza, invite families, and celebrate a job well done and the fresh new look as a team.

If All Else Fails, Own It

There is a chance that all efforts will be unsuccessful. An appeal to management may only generate a disappointing no. Employees may not be willing to give their own time or money for something they feel the agency should be responsible for. And while this can all feel disappointing, you still have the power to control your attitude about it.

Rather than focusing on all the downsides, find ways to use humor in the situation. Host an "ugliest office" contest or bring in ugly lamps to brighten dim workspaces. And, if all else fails, buy everyone red staplers. Regardless, make the space yours, no matter how ugly, and recognize that you can still do an excellent job even when the wallpaper is peeling behind your desk.

While an out-of-date office is not ideal, you still have options to make minor improvements. Using the above tips, you can sort out if those updates will be in the physical sense or simply how you choose to look at the space.

28. How Do Agency Managers Assess Employee Productivity in a Remote Work Environment?

My team's morale is down, and transitioning to a remote workforce is off to a bumpy start. We do not have any tracking software in place to monitor everyone's daily activities, and I don't know if I'm getting the straight scoop from employees. What are your feelings on activity tracking software?

The shift from in-office to remote work has presented a variety of challenges for insurance agencies. As so many made the transition overnight, being able to effectively move all operations from inside the same building into everyone's homes has been difficult for both agencies and their employees. We are living in unfamiliar and unprecedented circumstances. There is very little in our day-to-day work that is the same as it was a year ago. And as nice as it would be to march on with a "business as usual" mantra, that is just not an option because everything we do is far from normal.

As agencies and employees need to continue serving their clients, here are some tips for helping employees manage work in a remote environment.

Understand Individual Needs and Struggles

As many employees continue to work from home on a full-time or part-time basis, there is a continual adjustment for how they manage the situation in the best way possible. Individuals have found themselves tackling personal and work tasks all within the same space with little room for separation, and agency leaders are left trying to sort out how to accommodate individual needs and maintain efficiency.

With so many people simultaneously juggling their roles as parents, teachers, and full-time employees, there is an impact on both productivity and stress. As leaders, it is important to approach your employees with empathy and a desire to understand. Take time to ask questions and sort out the unique circumstances an employee is facing. By doing this, you can uncover their true struggles and start looking at options to work through those challenges.

Monitor and Adjust KPIs

While employees have made the shift to virtual work, more than just the environment has changed. Remote work combined with all the other activities taking place in the home have had an impact on the way employees work. Tasks may be happening in a different order, more or less frequently, and at different times of the day.

Understanding that employee working styles and behaviors have changed is an important factor to consider when reviewing current key performance indicators (KPIs). Continuing to measure productivity by the same standards despite all the changes can generate misleading results. Instead, take time to redefine and adjust productivity standards and the corresponding KPI's to understand when you are getting an accurate assessment of work completed and when employee intervention is needed.

Implement an Activity Tracking Software

As leaders, the need to pivot and adjust management style, communication, and employee monitoring is a daily hurdle that can quickly get overwhelming. If manually reviewing productivity gets to be too much, there are solutions available. Consider implementing an activity tracking software. This will help give you the desired oversight into employee working habits and assist in quantifying input and output.

There are several options available that you can use in a remote environment. You may even find some of these options useful for when and if employees return to the office. Knowing what information your agency needs will be an important first step to finding the right match. You can compare the features of different products through www.capterra.com and find the solution that best suits your agency's specific needs.

An agency's ability to adapt even when the road ahead is uncertain is critical to its long-term success. Using the tips above, you can make a few adjustments to the way you lead and monitor your virtual team to ensure everyone is moving forward together.

29. How Do We Improve Diversity and Inclusion in the Insurance Industry?

I am an agency owner, and I've been interviewing to hire a new producer to train up. There's a candidate I really like, but I'm fearful some of the prospects in our niche won't respond well to him being African American. Do I speak candidly about the potential challenges he might face or is that something I should keep to myself?

The insurance industry has been characterized in many less than complimentary ways regarding its lack of diversity. Sayings like "stale, pale, and male" and "good old boys club" are descriptions that have influenced opinions within and outside the industry. The truth is, the insurance industry has struggled with diversity and inclusion for a long time. Even as that tide has started to shift, there is still work required to shift mindsets inside and outside insurance.

While this can be a complicated topic that generates a lot of opinions and emotions, it is essential to be part of a movement that promotes a more diverse and inclusive industry.

Be Informed

Agency leaders must make sure they are looking at diversity issues within their agency and the industry. Ignoring diversity issues will negatively impact an agency in the future if it has not already. Not only is it a relevant issue that needs attention for it to improve, but it is also an essential part of the industry's future success. The next generation of employees looking at the insurance industry as a future career opportunity also seeks inclusive and diverse workplaces.

While there are no overnight solutions for improving diversity in the workplace, it is still essential to start by gaining an understanding of what role you and your agency play in taking steps toward improvements. Enlist a professional if needed. An equity, diversity, and inclusion (EDI) expert can help leaders and employees better understand and navigate EDI issues, identify their own biases, and provide tools for moving past those biases in a more positive direction. Being informed and taking appropriate action is not just one person's job, but it does start with leadership willing to take the first step.

Look for and Promote Diversity

Building a more diverse workforce can take more time and requires intention on behalf of the employer. Diversity within the insurance industry is a serious issue, and only paying it lip service by saying you and the agency support efforts to improve it no longer works. Taking action by hiring and promoting employees representing different cultures and lifestyles is needed to move the needle forward on this issue effectively. Ensuring that employees receive fair and equitable treatment is critical.

For example, not taking an idea seriously from a female but then immediately applauding the same information from a male employee leads to the continued marginalization of women. Promoting qualified leaders of diverse backgrounds and giving those leaders an equal seat at the table helps make sure that all voices are represented and heard.

Have an Open Dialogue—Don't Run from Tough Conversations

Equity, diversity, and inclusion are weighty topics that can be very challenging to discuss. However, ignoring it will not make it go away. Improvement starts with open dialogue. If you are not a minority, you may feel ill-equipped to be part of the conversation. But the truth is, admitting that you don't have first-hand experience with discrimination but you want to do what you can to help is a substantial first step. Creating a forum where employees feel safe sharing their questions and concerns is an equally important part of the equation.

Bringing in experts who can answer questions, provide feedback, and help employees tackle serious issues allows everyone an opportunity to learn and grow.

Ignoring or minimizing the issues the insurance industry faces when it comes to equity, diversity, and inclusion is a disservice to current employees and the next generation coming into this industry. Although these topics are difficult to tackle, doing your part to help reshape attitudes is critical to the insurance industry's continued growth.

30. How Do I Secure My Job When the Agency Is Making Cutbacks?

I am a newer account manager in the agency, and I am concerned about losing my job due to the economic downturn. What would you suggest I do to protect my job at this time?

A major threat to job security is the long-term impact of COVID-19 on the economy. The insurance industry is certainly not insulated from this. While particular niches your agency serves may be able to weather or even succeed amid the pandemic, others have suffered unsustainable blows to their income, leaving them with no choice but to close their doors. As businesses close, their need for insurance goes away as well. This sequence of events can undoubtedly impact agencies' bottom lines, leaving owners with tough choices to make when it comes to cutting back expenses, which can often mean layoffs.

While there's never any employment guarantee, here are some tips you can use to create more job security for yourself amid uncertainty.

Be a Team Player

Many agencies are struggling on so many levels amid an ever-evolving pandemic. One significant challenge has been employee time as many continue to tackle virtual work and virtual school for children who cannot return to a traditional school environment. While managers continue to accommodate employee needs as best as possible, clients still expect and need service.

Some employees may require more help than others to meet their clients' needs. If you have time or skills that could be of value, raise your hand and offer to help. This willingness to pitch in fills a critical need of the agency and allows the agency to maintain service standards that clients have come to expect.

Step Up Your Performance

Agency leaders must tackle multiple priorities in unprecedented circumstances. As the situation around the pandemic continues to ebb and flow, managers need to balance staff needs and availability against tightening budgets. Long story short, employees' demands far exceed the availability of several valuable resources in many agencies.

Finding a way to minimize those concerns in your work demonstrates ownership, responsibility, and respect for your work and the agency's needs. Going above and beyond to support your clients' needs and pitching in where you can elsewhere provides much-needed relief to leadership.

Be Aware of Options in the Market

As some agencies that experience shrinkage are left with no option but to make cuts, others will find ways to overcome the pandemic's adversity and grow. As hard as it may be to think about leaving an agency you call home, you may not have a choice if there are layoffs. Planning for an unfortunate scenario like a layoff is not assuming the worst, but it does help you prepare to handle the potential situation.

To gain a better understanding of the hiring market, get active on social media, especially LinkedIn. Connect with other insurance professionals and agencies. Stay up to date on job postings and know that your opportunities are not limited to geographic location. Remote work is more prevalent in the insurance industry than ever before, which means there are no restrictions to where you could potentially find employment should the need arise.

While there is no way to completely eliminate the risk of unemployment, these tips will put you in a better position to have continued success in uncertain times.

31. What Should an Employee Do If They Have a Romantic Interest in a Coworker?

My office had an off-site, team-building event at Topgolf. A coworker from another department and I really hit it off and ended up kissing. I don't think anyone noticed because everyone had a bit too much to drink, but I'm stuck wondering what to do next. It's been a couple of weeks and my coworker and I haven't even talked about what happened. I don't want to mess up the opportunity with this company, but I really like her. What should I do?

A job in insurance can sometimes involve long days spent working side by side with other colleagues and occasional events in the evening. As coworkers spend more time together, they may begin to share more life experiences and build a personal relationship. This situation can sometimes be the perfect recipe for two employees to develop stronger feelings and a desire to pursue a romantic relationship.

Office romances are nothing new, but there is a good chance that this is unfamiliar territory for most people. Before the relationship gets too serious, there are a few essential things you will want to keep in mind.

Make Sure You Understand the Agency Policy

Some agencies have stringent policies that prohibit employees from dating one another. And if the feelings are one-sided, continuing to pursue any non-work-related relationship with a coworker can quickly turn into a harassment issue. You must understand any guidelines the agency has in place and proceed accordingly. If the agency has banned inner-office dating and you decide to continue the relationship anyway, you will want to make sure you are fully aware of the consequences.

Be Honest About the Relationship

Honesty does not mean you are required to make an announcement to the company after the first date. However, attempting to hide a romance in the long-term can make the rest of your coworkers uncomfortable, spark unnecessary office gossip, and generate a lack of trust once people find out about the relationship.

Explaining the relationship to a supervisor or manager first is the best place to start. Your manager should be able to provide clarification about any company policies or office protocols you may not be aware of. Informing them of the relationship also allows them to assess how closely you and the other person work together and make necessary arrangements.

Lastly, a supervisor should be able to give some guidance as to how to let the others in the office know about the relationship.

Discuss Workplace Boundaries

Whether the relationship is going well or there is some stress involved, the rest of your colleagues should not get caught up in the circumstances of your relationship on any given day. In other words, the status of your relationship should never interfere with work.

Talking through and setting rules and boundaries for work is essential on so many different levels. Healthy boundaries will ensure that you are conscientious of your coworkers' feelings. It will also help you focus on your work and maintain your professionalism. And if things do not work out with the relationship, having established boundaries will make a post-breakup adjustment a little smoother.

Romantic relationships with a coworker can be tricky to navigate. Following these guidelines will help ensure you're able to keep both work and romance in check.

32. What Should Agency Owners Look for When Hiring?

What are the top qualities and qualifications you are looking for right now in candidates who are brand new to the industry hires as well as those with a few years of experience?

The insurance industry's job market has been competitive for many years and continues to get more aggressive. The pressure to bring new talent is being felt at many agencies regardless of size or location. And while there may be several responses to a job posting, not every potential hire is going to be the right hire for the agency.

Here are four essential characteristics an agency owner will want to look for during the hiring process:

- **Critical thinking**. Individuals willing and able to think outside of the box will bring new ideas to the table. When an employee can tap into critical thinking skills, they will approach their work differently than others. When problems and challenges arise, they can look at those things from different angles and generate creative solutions.

- **Flexibility and adaptability.** As much as some things remain very much the same in insurance, many things change with how an agency needs to operate. Whether it is adopting new technology or revising processes, many agencies frequently evaluate, restrategize, and pivot when needed.

- An individual who is too rigid and resistant to change will create a lot of work for others and be less productive. However, open-minded individuals who are prepared to make adjustments will help move the organization closer to its goals.

- **Desire to learn.** A willingness to always be a student of the industry is critical. The insurance industry can be a complicated world with an overwhelming amount of information, even at its most basic level. Insurance continues to evolve, whether in regard to client needs and demands or the way carriers do business. A candidate prepared to stay on top of new developments and information will be a tremendous asset to the agency and its clients.

- **Emotional intelligence.** Every component of the insurance industry is relationship driven. Whether it is from agency to carrier, employee to client, or employee to employee, relationships matter.

Individuals who possess a high degree of emotional intelligence will be empathetic and understanding. This characteristic will allow them to build strong relationships with clients and coworkers alike.

Experience may be desired but should not be the primary focus when assessing a new potential hire for the agency. Seeking out an individual who embodies the right qualities and skills will set the agency and its employees up for continued growth and success.

33. What Resources Should Agencies Provide to New Employees to Set Them Up for Success?

I am the newest employee at a small agency. I am spending time with each of the other employees to learn the ropes. It has been tough to keep up as each person does things differently and there are no procedures to follow. Is there anything I can do to get all this information organized so that I'm actually able to learn my job?

Workflows and procedures can often be a second thought and take a back seat to the actual work required to service agency clients. Without clear guidelines, employees are doing their jobs to the best of their knowledge but are very likely doing things their own way. When this happens, employees can miss essential steps in the process, which can generate inconsistent results.

Here are some insights into four critical resources every employee needs to be effective.

Centralized Access

Everyone needs to have access to the same set of information. If information is currently on individual computers, this can create a couple of issues:

- Not everyone has access to each other's computers.
- Employees may not be using the most updated version of the document.

A central drive can be used house workflows and other resources like carrier underwriting guidelines, important contacts, or commonly used forms and applications.

By creating a centralized database, all reference documents that employees should be using are in one place that is easy to access and always up to date.

Clear Step-by-Step Procedures

If your agency is creating procedures for the first time or updating its procedures, invest some time to thoroughly document your procedures into a usable format.

Spend time with employees to understand each step they are taking as they work through different processes. Whether it is new business, renewals, audits, or endorsements, there are specific steps involved to make those processes work from start to finish. Pull all the individual feedback together to create one singular set of steps for each process. These processes include detailed steps and screenshots.

Video Workflows

Once you can identify each step in the process, take it to the next level by recording the procedures. Employees joining the agency are accustomed to digital learning as they have been consuming video their entire lives.

Using a video recording software like Zoom, your team can quickly and easily build a digital resource library for all workflows. Recorded workflows provide a significant benefit as employees can view them whenever and as many times as needed. And each time they view it, they are guaranteed to get the same consistent information.

Regularly review and update. Workflows will need to be modified from time to time. You may need to adapt workflows in response to functionality in the agency management system, changes that trickle down from the carriers, or many other reasons. Rather than making constant changes and creating confusion, schedule regular review checkpoints throughout the year. Examine current procedures, get suggestions from staff regarding improvements, and update accordingly.

Collecting all these pieces of information can be time consuming in the beginning. However, having agency processes documented and accessible to all employees will be a significant improvement when it comes to training new staff and driving consistency across the organization.

34. How Should Agencies Prepare for the AMS Conversion Process?

The agency I work at recently went through an agency management system conversion. The training time was a little aggressive and rushed. Since then, the day-to-day workload at the agency has been brutal. Employees are struggling to adjust to the new system, work is getting backlogged, and the frustration is being felt across the organization. How do we course correct from here?

Agency management systems (AMS) present a high cost to the agency. They are complicated systems that require time, attention, and skill to ensure that they are being managed and used effectively within an agency. Any agency that has been through an AMS conversion can quickly tell you that it never entirely goes as planned. It is a challenging process with an unending number of factors that impact every operation in the agency. In short, converting to an AMS may be the most stressful technology upgrades an agency has to make.

Here are tips to prepare agency staff for the AMS conversion process:

Assess the Project's Scope, Expenses, and Budget

Agencies must have as much information as possible before beginning the AMS conversion process. Gather details from the vendor regarding the training, timelines, and costs.

- **Training.** The vendor should provide a proposed training plan that should detail the types of training available, whether it is live webinars, on-demand webinars, or in-person instruction. It is also essential to get details regarding additional training options the vendor could provide should this be an option the agency needs to provide to employees.

- **Timeline.** The integration process will likely be extensive with different programming, data transfers, and other setups throughout the process. Be sure to have a complete understanding of what needs to happen at each stage and the associated timeline for all steps of the process.

- **Costs.** Agencies should have a clear understanding of the cost of the system itself and the cost associated with the onboarding process, including programming, implementation, formal training, and *additional* training employees may need.

Assign a Project Manager

Any significant project that an agency undergoes needs a person leading the charge. The AMS conversion process is no different. This project manager will need to have a comprehensive understanding of the old and new systems. They will also need to have extensive knowledge regarding the steps required in the conversion process. The project manager will need to be the primary contact between the vendor and the agency and remain in continual communication with the vendor during all stages. Taking time to develop this insight will allow them to manage the process and communicate the action plan to the rest of the agency more effectively.

Hire an Implementation Specialist

Whether or not an agency has a project manager assigned from within the organization, an implementation specialist can be a tremendous asset during the conversion process. An implementation specialist will have extensive knowledge of the AMS and can help provide valuable insight into the system's nuances. They will also be able to give specific direction as to steps that need to be taken at all stages of the process to ensure the conversion goes as smoothly as possible. This type of service does come with a hefty price tag, so agencies need to be clear on the cost upfront.

Invest Time in Data Cleanup

Many of the issues that rise to the surface after a system conversion can result from bad data. Whether it is the incorrect use of data fields within the applications or failure to deactivate old files, bad data in one system will slide into the new system and create headaches for everyone. Taking extra time to clean up before moving information from the old system to the new will prevent a lot of stress down the line. Agencies can also outsource this work rather than burden agency staff with the cleanup tasks.

Opt for an Extended Preparation Timeline

There is no Undo button once an agency hits go on a system conversion. It is much better to take extra time before the conversion rather than go through the stress of trying to remedy issues after the fact. Opting for extended preparation time will allow the agency additional time for data cleanup and training, preventing a lot of stress when the new AMS goes live.

The conversion process is not an easy one, and 100 percent of the headaches are not preventable. Taking these steps should help agencies have a better experience when it is time to upgrade.

35. How Do Agency Leaders Successfully Develop and Execute Agency Initiatives and Goals?

The last few years, agency owners have brought the leadership team together to develop the strategic plan. There is a lot of good discussion and good ideas shared, but we end up with over thirty initiatives. We try to attack the whole list, and efforts are very scattered. I think we should take a different approach. What can I do to help ownership focus when setting goals for the agency?

Goal-setting is critical to leading an agency that remains focused on future growth and success.

These planning sessions can be full of creative, outside-of-the-box ideas where "anything is possible."

While it can be easy to get carried away with massive lists of goals and to-dos, there must be steps taken to evaluate and select goals that will have the most significant impact.

How do agency leaders identify and execute goals for the organization?

- **Ensure goals align with the company vision.** The company vision is the agency roadmap to success, and all goals should reflect it. Suppose there are initiatives on the list unrelated to the vision. In that case, there is a good chance that working on those things will not move the company forward and will create a distraction from those goals that should be taking priority.

- **Pause and reflect.** Examining the last year's results is an important part of determining steps for the future. Review initiatives from the prior year. Was the agency able to meet or exceed all goals? When it comes to the goals which the agency was able to meet, how was that achieved? In those areas where the agency fell short, what improvements does the agency need to make those a reality?

- Taking the time to evaluate what has worked or not worked in the past is a great way to make sure you don't repeat past mistakes and continue to push forward with those strategies that have served the agency well.

- **Quality over quantity.** There may be a long list of ideas generated when everyone is collaborating and brainstorming, but it is essential to evaluate all ideas, keep those that help the agency make its most significant strides towards accomplishing the company vision.

- Taking on too many initiatives at one time will prevent the agency from focusing its efforts and resources, which sets everyone up for failure. Those goals that don't make the cut this year can always be resurrected for consideration the following year.

- **Define steps needed to make goals a reality.** Identifying the goals is an integral part of the process, but creating an action plan is even more critical. For every initiative selected for the agency, there needs to be a path from where the organization is now to where it wants to be. Ensure that all employees involved are clear on the steps needed to take the goals from words on a piece of paper to active initiatives for the organization.

- **Know what success looks like.** Accountability remains a critical component to ensuring the agency continues to move toward the designated goals. For every initiative the agency has established, there should be KPIs (key performance indicators). The KPIs are the mechanism by which agency leaders will evaluate the agency's progress toward its goals and make necessary adjustments.

Transparent communication to the entire organization throughout the process will keep everyone engaged and moving in the same direction.

Having ambitious goals for an agency is the sign of a growth-minded organization. Taking the time to be deliberate and intentional about identifying goals and the steps needed to achieve them will allow the agency to continue building a path toward success.

36. What Criteria Should Agency Leaders Use When Evaluating Continuing Education for Insurance?

An employee on my team wants to earn a professional designation in the next two years. He has made a few attempts but has not had any success. The time and money involved in sending him are starting to add up. Does it make sense for the agency to continuing spending money for this employee to earn a designation?

Continuing education comes with the territory for insurance professionals, and one option that continues to be popular in the industry is professional designation courses. There are several choices available, each with its own requirements as well as pros and cons.

Given that there are so many options, what do agencies need to know when employees pursue a professional designation?

Course Subjects

Professional designations consist of a series of courses covering a wide variety of topics. Insurance professionals attend a set of courses and take the exams to earn one or more of these designations.

While this can seem like a great plan on the surface, there is a problem. There are so many subjects involved that it is easy for an employee to spend time learning something that does not relate to their job. In other words, they are spending hours on a class that has no applicable information for when they return to the office. This process can be a frustrating exercise for the employee and a waste of agency dollars.

Quality of Curriculum

Materials for classes are not reviewed and updated as often as they should be. The employee is then at risk of being taught inaccurate information and passing misinformation onto clients. To rectify this, agencies need to take proactive steps to ensure information employees are learning holds up to current case law.

Testing Requirements

here is a testing component to all professional designations. The problem that can come into play is the accuracy of the test-grading systems. Guidelines regarding test review are not well regulated. This lack of regulation can lead to an employee falsely failing a course and having to repeat the work all over again to continue working towards the designation.

Some employees may struggle with testing in general. Their low comfort level with tests may cause stress that prevents them from getting everything they should out of the course.

Logistics

Designation courses are typically offered in a traditional classroom with online education recently gaining popularity. The classroom option can present a challenge as far as the location where the course is. There will generally be travel required for employees to attend.

The online option may present challenges for making sure that the right technology is available for the employee to connect and comply with all privacy and proxy requirements during test-taking.

Whatever option the employee selects, there is a time limit associated with earning the designation.

Employees need to be sure they can fulfill the assigned time frame requirements or risk losing credit toward the designation.

Cost

There are a couple of factors involved when assessing the cost of a designation. Each course has a fee for the class itself. Once completing the series of courses and earning the designation, agencies will need to continue paying for annual dues and additional courses for the employee to maintain their designation.

Continuing education for the sake of logging credit hours or earning a designation is not going to yield useful results. Instead, an emphasis on quality learning that elevates agent professionalism and knowledge will benefit both the employee, the client, and the agency.

37. How Can Agency Employees Overcome Personality Differences?

The head of our IT department is extremely smart but can be difficult to work with. When employees ask for help, his responses can come off as short and rude. It has gotten to the point that employees won't ask for help. This tension is leading to employees not getting what they need to complete their work, and it cannot be avoided any longer. How do I get the team past this so that we can all get back to working together the way we need to?

Each employee within an agency is a little bit different from the next. Having a staff of individuals who work and think differently can be great when people can collaborate and play off of each other's strengths. However, some individual temperaments can be so contrasting that it can cause friction. When this happens, problems can arise that are increasingly disruptive to work.

While employees do not need to be best friends, there is a certain level of decency and respect required to work together effectively and without being miserable. Here are a few tips for helping employees move beyond conflicting personalities so everyone can get back to work.

Identify and Appreciate Individual Contributions

The different roles within an agency require different attributes of the person doing the job. Technical proficiencies or interpersonal skills may position an employee as a perfect fit in one job instead of another. When employees find themselves in conflict, they may disregard the importance of another's role. When this happens, it is critical to take a step back and look at how each position within the agency plays an integral part in helping the organization achieve everything it needs.

By taking this time to pause and examine each role's function, employees can see how other individuals' skills and expertise contribute to the continued success of the agency.

Emphasize a Shared Goal

When disagreements occur between employees, they can get caught up in the emotions of conflict. They may focus their attention on the problem and avoid working with the employee they deem responsible for the issues, which creates a distraction from work.

To get work back on track, establish commonalities. Whether it's the overall agency objectives or a specific project that requires everyone's cooperation and contributions, pull the focus back on a shared goal. Bring attention to what brings employees together to minimize the divisive activity that is pushing them apart.

Diagnose the Root Cause of the Problem

Conflict rarely is what it appears to be on the surface. More often, there are underlying issues smoldering beneath the surface. Disagreements between employees can arise from a variety of different reasons. Conflicts can arise because of a lack of training for one employee and another feeling burdened to make up for that coworker's underperformance. Two employees may have misaligned expectations. Sometimes faulty communication can cause problems. And other times, personality types can create tension between employees. Left unaddressed, or incorrectly addressed, resentment can quickly spark.

It's essential to have open conversations with those involved to unearth where the problems are stemming from. Once you have figured out the cause, you can identify a solution. Solutions could be additional training to increase proficiency or a commitment to more precise communication in the future. If there are conflicting personalities, consider having employees complete the Enneagram Personality Profile test. Feedback from this test will provide insight for the employees on how they think, process, and respond to challenges by providing a baseline for better problem-solving in the future.

Address Toxic Behavior

Conflict is one thing, but toxic behavior is much more severe.

Regardless of what assets an employee may bring to an agency, it is not worth allowing them to create a toxic environment. Tolerating this type of behavior can quickly drive down the morale of others, erode agency culture, and cause good employees to move on to a workplace where they feel cared for and valued.

If an employee is divisive and refuses to change the way they interact with others, make sure to have a plan to let them go.

While conflict is inevitable, it doesn't have to be destructive. When people who behave and work differently come together to solve disagreements productively, conflict can help create stronger teams.

38. How Can Agencies Streamline the Quoting Process?

I handle the commercial lines online rating for the agency. There are producers who have a habit of sending last-minute and incomplete requests. I try to accommodate these requests, but the constant follow up takes so much time and also means someone else is not getting what they need. I've reexplained the correct process to the producers, but nothing changes. Is there anything I can do to get this process running smoother?

New business acquisition is critical to the growth of an agency. However, in many cases it is full of inefficient and inconsistent processes. Without the right tools and guidelines, producers can easily find themselves creating their own way of doing things, leaving the next person in the process without the necessary details to manage the quoting process.

While this can be frustrating, here are a few tips every agency can implement to take the friction out of the quoting process.

Keep the Process Simple

Simplifying your process is not intended to create a free pass for not doing the work. However, the human brain is always looking for the path of least resistance. Ensuring the data gathering process is as easy as possible is suitable for both the producer and the client and will help you get complete information consistently.

Overloading the process with requests for unnecessary information will lead to more questions, frustration, and a lack of cooperation. Instead, make sure that any forms used for gathering client data are clean and straightforward. Eliminate any questions (or entire sections) asking for impertinent or duplicate information.

Set a Standard for Collecting Complete Information

This statement may seem a bit like stating the obvious. The agent must ask the right questions and obtain the necessary details. Trying to bypass this work is a disservice to the client and the agency.

And if a prospect is not willing to provide all the information needed, there is a good chance they aren't interested enough to see the process through. However, if they are engaged, agents need to be prepared to do a thorough analysis. Gather sound information to ensure that your prospective client understands their risk and provide the appropriate coverage for the insured's exposures. Look at this as the first step to building a client relationship.

Be Prepared for Questions

Even when it seems like you've dotted every *i* and crossed every *t*, questions will come up. You will need to field questions from underwriters and individuals at the agency reviewing the submission before it goes out. While the risk may seem simple and straightforward on the surface, there could be unique characteristics or concerns that require clarification for the underwriter.

To ensure the quoting process keeps moving forward, confirm there are communication protocols set up for every person in the process. Whether it's letting the underwriter know who they should contact with questions, who will communicate with the insured, or the timeline for responses, setting a standard will maintain open communication lines, reduce confusion, and keep everyone involved on the same page.

Document the Process and Address Problems

All procedures in an agency require documentation and auditing. Clearly defined and documented processes create a reference point for employees to go back to when needing a reminder. Auditing establishes a system for confirming the use of the procedures.

Thorough documentation will help you ensure that the process is staying on time, information from the producer is complete, and communication is remaining clear and responsive throughout the process. These are all critical components to making sure that the right system is in place. If problems are evident in auditing or issues brought to light by employees, it's essential to address and correct early.

Producers want to grow their book and continue building new relationships. Designing proper processes will help ensure that everyone is working together to make that happen.

39. How Do Agencies Regain Control of Agency Billing Issues?

I currently work in the accounting department reconciling agency bill premiums. About half of our commercial accounts have at least one line of business currently billed from the agency. About 25 percent of that business is overdue month after month. These are significant dollars the agency is holding the bag on each month. Is there anything we should be doing to better manage this payment delinquency issue?

Agencies may have to provide an agency bill vs direct bill option for certain insureds. Utilizing the agency bill option can be valuable for meeting clients' needs. However, it can become problematic if agencies do not monitor it and clients take advantage of it. Left unchecked, what should be another tool to better service clients can quickly turn into an accounts receivable nightmare.

Without the right practices in place, an agency can find themselves fighting an unpaid premium battle. Here are a few keys to managing the process to prevent and correct delinquent agency bill premium issues?

Address Payment Issues Early

Bad habits develop quickly and can be hard to break. If the insured gets away with it a few times, there is a good chance the behavior will continue. Failing to check in with the client when payment is past due sends a message that it is acceptable for them not to pay premiums on time. The only one feeling any pain in this situation is the agency.

Getting payments back on track requires discussing the problem with clients sooner rather than later. Putting the conversation off will only make it worse. Reaching out to the insured and expressing concerns directly and respectfully works best. Simply calling and letting them know you are paying attention may be enough to correct the problem. It is essential to explain the expectations for timely premium payment. The conversation may feel a little awkward and uncomfortable, but it is critical to ensuring that the agency does not start getting treated like a lending institution.

Get the Client's Attention with Prompt Action

When premiums go unpaid, agencies are within their rights to proceed with the cancellation process. Issuing an "Intent to Cancel" notice to additional interests and certificate holders can be enough to get the client's attention and let them know you are serious about payment issues.

For example, your insured is a contractor who is repeatedly paying late, and the agency is left chasing down premium month after month. When the payment goes past due and the cancellation process begins, the agency can then email cancellation notices to all the certificate holders. The contractor finds themselves unable to get on a job site, which leads to a call back to the agency to find out what is going on. Now that you have gotten the insured's attention, you can reiterate the agency's obligation to notify. Taking this step may feel extreme, but it will get the insured's attention and may also be the most effective way to resolve payment issues from that point forward.

Equip Staff for Difficult Conversations

The account manager, producer, or someone from accounting must have the proper set of information going into conversations with clients about payment issues. This conversation could include reminding the insured of the company policy, informing them of a final due date to avoid cancellation, or leveraging a manager's authority in the agency. Providing employees with talking points will allow them to be clear with insureds and keep the conversation focused.

Have a Written Policy

Developing an agency policy for both agency employees and insureds can help remove ambiguity and keep both sides of the equation on the same page. Outlining terms for billing and payment clarifies precisely how the agency views and handles agency bill premiums. When and if issues arise, employees can quickly reference the document to remind insureds of the agency's stance on payment and quickly eliminate confusion and pushback.

Unpaid agency bill premiums will negatively impact client relationships and agency finances. Following these tips will help agencies get both on track.

40. How Do Agencies Effectively Use the Reporting Functions of the AMS?

I handle all administrative duties for our agency management system and am responsible for running all reports for the organization. Every month I run reports, share results, and provide details on errors and issues identified in the reports. Month after month I report the same errors. The problems are clear to me, but how do I get leadership to do something about it?

Insurance agencies rely on reports to review and track performance across the organization. Reports provide insight that agency leaders need to compare the agency's current status against their goals and make appropriate strategic decisions to keep the organization progressing. The problem that arises, however, is that reports are often difficult to understand and interpret.

System-generated reports are also at high risk for errors due to the data that is in the system.

What can agencies do to make sure they are using reports in the AMS effectively?

Identify Critical Information

Before going through the setup process, leadership needs to identify what they need to see from a reporting standpoint. Without defining this, agencies can quickly get caught up in reporting for the sake of reporting. The first step is understanding the strategic initiatives, timeline, and progress benchmarks required to confirm if the agency is on track.

This clarification will provide the direction needed to set up reports properly.

For example, an agency has a growth goal of 10 percent. Monthly reporting should provide feedback on new business, lost business, and retention. Every report should tie back to a specific goal. Anything outside of this is potentially information that has no impact on growth and performance, which only creates a distraction. Narrowing down reporting to correlate precisely with the agency's vision allows leadership to focus on the data that matters most. If it's not valuable to the agency, delete it!

Confirm Reports Settings Are Correct

AMSs typically come stocked with a variety of prebuilt reports. However, these are one-size-fits-most templates and using them without any modifications will likely provide inaccurate results. Given that every agency makes some level of customization to their AMS to fit their business's specific needs, the reports will need to be customized as well. Report criteria need to be accurate to ensure that reports are producing valid information. To handle this most effectively, agencies will want to assign someone within the organization to oversee the reports' setup and production. It is also a good idea for this individual to work directly with the AMS company or an outside consultant who has a deep understanding of the AMS.

A method for verifying data and checking for errors is critical as well. Data will be flawed, and systems will fail. Develop a process for identifying errors before they become agency performance gospel.

Convert Data into an Easy-to-Understand, Actionable Format

AMS reports can get out of control very quickly—spreadsheets of data with columns and rows for miles. This information becomes overwhelming for leaders. Trying to dissect the massive amount of totals and percentages can take hours.

The person or team in charge of managing the agency reports will also need to simplify all of the details in a format that is easy to look at and understand. Color-coded charts and graphs with a legend and even a brief narrative will summarize mounds of data into something usable. When the information is pulled together in an easy-to-use format, leadership can quickly see results, compare against goals, and start making strategic decisions.

Create and Implement a Plan for Cleaning and Auditing Data

Reports generated from the AMS are only as good as the information entered into the system. The saying *garbage in, garbage out* applies here. Inaccurate data leads to bad reports. Erroneous reports generate incorrect information, which gets submitted to leadership. Using inaccurate information leads to misinformed decisions.

Bad data can cause several issues in an agency's operations, including inaccurate information on clients, policy limits, premiums, revenue, and other policy details. Not only does this create an issue with reporting, but it can also become an Errors and Omissions issue for the agency.

Data cleanup projects can be very time consuming but are a worthwhile investment in the long run. Problems with your data stemming from a misuse of a data field or missing information will impact reporting and anything else generated from the system. Consider outsourcing or hiring temps or interns to take on the project.

Agencies will also need to implement auditing practices. Auditing information in the system on an ongoing basis is critical to keeping the AMS functioning in a way that allows the agency to use it as a tool that helps the agency operate more efficiently.

Without the right processes and procedures to support reporting functions, the AMS becomes an expensive data warehouse. Putting the above pointers into practice will allow agencies to utilize their system better and start leveraging reports to make well-informed decisions for the organization, driving continued success.

41. How Do Agencies Offer Benefits That Are Fair to Employees?

The agency I work at offers flexible scheduling to employees so they can attend things for their kids like doctor's appointments, school programs, and sporting events. I think this is great, but I am single with no children and therefore, not being offered any options for a flexible schedule. Just because I don't have kids does not mean that I don't have other things going on. Is there anything I can do to lobby for the rights of single folks?

The desire to achieve a balance between projects at work and obligations at home has been a relevant topic of conversation for a long time. When employees can achieve this, they are less stressed and happier with their employer, which usually means they are more productive and more likely to stick with their job. Many benefits offered have primarily focused on employees with a family, leaving employees with different personal circumstances feeling cheated.

Statistics show that people are getting married later or choosing other lifestyles, but benefits offered by employers are failing to catch up to more modern lifestyles. Here are a few modifications agencies can make to their benefits package to help all employees feel supported.

Flexible Scheduling

Allowing employees to create a schedule outside of the traditional workweek continues to grow in popularity in agencies of all sizes. A recent survey shows that many companies still only offer this benefit to employees with children. It is essential to acknowledge that employees who do not have children still desire flexibility. Most employees have interests and responsibilities outside of work, and some of those may occasionally interfere with regular working hours. Limiting this benefit only to employees with children can be frustrating to those that do not.

To make this option fair to staff regardless of their family situation, consider broadening the guidelines to be more inclusive of all employees. Options like a flat number of hours per week or per month with set expectations about work completion and a plan to cover clients' needs during business hours will allow more employees to benefit from a flexible schedule.

Family Leave

Employer-paid family leave is a voluntary benefit that many companies continue to offer only to employees for life events like the birth or adoption of a new child or care for a sick child. However, as of the end of 2019, the Family Caregiver Alliance reports that 39.8 million people in the US are caregivers for adults with a disability or illness.

If the family leave policy at your agency is defined by the traditional guidelines of parent-child relationships, it's essential to expand this. Whether it is an adult child or an aging parent who cannot take care of themselves independently, there is a good chance that employees within your agency are designated caregivers to an adult in their lives.

Bereavement Leave

Many agency handbooks contain language for bereavement, restricting it to family members only. Even though many employees may not currently be married or have plans to ever take a walk down the aisle, policies for the benefit remain written to accommodate traditional family setups. The reality is that employees have significant relationships outside of the normal spousal or familial ones. An employee may wish to take leave following the death of a partner, significant other, or even a close friend to whom the employee is not related.

Reviewing and broadening this to make sure it works for all lifestyles will ensure that employees can focus on what they need when dealing with a loved one's death instead of forcing them to utilize paid time off or request an exception.

When employees feel like their personal and professional needs are being addressed by their employer, they feel cared for. By making modifications to the benefits package to be more conducive to different lifestyles, agencies benefit not only by having more satisfied employees but also positioning themselves to attract new talent seeking an employer that can meet their needs regardless of their marital or familial status.

42. Should I Offer Unlimited Vacation to My Employees?

I handle phone screens and coordinate the interview process for new applicants. When I discuss the agency benefits package with the applicant, I get feedback that we are not keeping pace with other agencies they have interviewed with. The primary benefits they seem to be looking for is unlimited vacation. This is not anything the agency has considered offering, but should we?

The idea of unlimited vacation gained popularity a few years ago as large corporations like Netflix, Hubspot, and Linked in made national headlines for offering this benefit to employees. And while it may sound like a great option to get the attention of potential new hires, there are many different factors to evaluate before adding it to your agency's benefits package.

Before implementing unlimited vacation at your agency, be sure to consider the following carefully.

Unlimited Vacation Is Vague and Confusing

The word unlimited indicates that there is no limit to how much vacation an employee can take.

However, it is not quite that simple. Agencies still need to have a written vacation policy. Without clear guidelines, agencies may find employees are confused and frustrated. Depending on an employee's role at the agency, they may need to be accessible to clients. Without a clear understanding of the expectations for vacation days, employees may find themselves answering calls and emails for clients rather than completely stepping away from work.

Developing a policy that defines vacation, explains how work should be shifted, and offers employees the flexibility they need will go further in building a culture that helps employees achieve success at work while pursuing fulfilling activities outside of the office.

Unlimited Vacation May Not Add Value for Employees

Studies show that employees do not use unlimited vacation just because it is available. The average vacation limit in the US is currently around two weeks, and most employees do not even use that limited amount. Studies show that 768 million hours of vacation went unused in the US in 2018. Agency employees are at risk of underutilizing their vacation days even when given unlimited time off.

Instead of offering an unlimited amount, put effort into getting employees to take a minimum number of days off. When employees are encouraged, even required, to take healthy breaks from work to recharge, they are happier, healthier, and more productive.

Unlimited Vacation Is Not a Hands-Free Policy

Unlimited vacation does not put managers off the hook of monitoring vacation usage. There are still valid reasons for knowing who is using vacation and when they are using it. While the primary concern may not be whether employees will abuse the privilege and not show up to work, it certainly is a risk. You can quickly become overwhelmed with micromanaging vacations in your attempts to ensure that clients are receiving service and other team members are not being overwhelmed while supporting a healthy balance in scheduling.

An alternative option is to maintain the current vacation policy and leave the door open to discuss additional vacation on a case-by-case basis. This option allows managers an opportunity to make sure struggling employees aren't putting themselves further behind while also rewarding top performers who may need an extra day or two in particular circumstances.

While unlimited vacation might appear to be a great option on the surface, it can create complications that make more work for managers and fail to deliver value to employees. Investing time and money into resources that provide the benefits employees need and want will go a long way in creating a happier agency that attracts and retains top-quality employees.

43. How Do You Get a Producer's Performance Back on Track When Sales Dip?

We're having a performance issue with one of our producers and can't seem to get him on the right track. What part of the sales process do you think we should be monitoring, and how would you suggest going about it without micromanaging?

No two producers are alike, and this is apparent in the way they go about selling. Each producer will develop their selling style based on their personality and the type of client they are pursuing. As much as producers need flexibility and freedom to add their unique flavor to what they do, not every choice they make will generate the desired results. There may come a time when their methods are not just ineffective but detrimental to their growth.

Convincing a producer to change their selling habits may not be the easiest task, but here are some tips to break things down and get to the root of the problem so the producer can get back to doing what they do best.

Assess the Problem

Once a decline in performance becomes apparent, it's essential to take a closer look. Rather than examining just one or two months, look at sales data over an extended period, perhaps six to twelve months. Looking at that information should help identify whether this is a blip on the radar or a downward trend.

For example, if you review the past year of sales data and see the producer has been on track with their sales goal for ten of the past twelve months, there's a good chance that this is just a temporary issue. And if there's a bigger problem starting to brew, you have hopefully identified it early enough that you can start encouraging the producer to turn things around. However, if you look at the last year and see that there has been a steady downward trend, this is more problematic. Declining performance could indicate that the producer is not as invested in their career as they should be, and it may be time to move them on to a new opportunity.

Dissect the Process

While every producer might put their own spin on the sales process, there should be codified steps to guide them through prospecting to closing the sale. While reviewing the process, do not assume the issues are impacting only one individual. Chances are, the process may not be working for any of the producers; it just hasn't become problematic from a sales standpoint, yet.

Each part of the process, whether it is pipeline management, data gathering, submission and quote review, or proposal presentation, is vital to making a sale. Overall, looking at each team members' individual processes will allow you to review multiple datasets, identify trends, create benchmarks, and detect problems.

Revise and Execute

Finding the issues in the process is only half the battle. Once you have identified the pitfalls, you must make necessary adjustments. You may need to lean on your creativity to come up with solutions. Ask your producers for input on what could work more effectively to generate buy-in when it comes time to implement those changes. Recognize that adopting a new or revised process will be a work in progress and should not deter you from executing those changes.

Allow producers time to adjust and adapt to the new process and leave the door open for discussion should there be concerns and tweaks needed along the way.

While performance issues can seem like one thing on the surface, there is usually more to the story. Taking the time to dive deeper and truly understand the problem will help producers find more success, which will always lead to more success for the agency.

44. Should Agencies Invest in Lead Lists?

2020 has been tough for growth, but the agency where I work has decided not to adjust production goals. I have asked to buy lead lists to generate more business, but the agency is rejecting my proposal based on poor experiences in the past. What are your thoughts on lead lists?

Sourcing enough leads to keep the new business pipeline full and new business goals on track can often be a challenge for insurance agencies. Maintaining a health stream of prospects, whether this is impacted by the niche a producer specializes in, the type of insurance they sell, or the restrictions of the agency's geographic location, is imperative to the sales process.

When it comes to keeping a full bank of prospects year round, lead lists are one option available to insurance agencies. Lead lists can be a bit of a gamble, so before buying, here are a few things to consider.

Know Your Client Type

The clients you typically work with and pursue likely have some similar characteristics. At the very least, you can categorize them into personal lines or commercial lines. Lead lists are often more effective for personal lines than for commercial lines. With personal lines lead lists, you are generally going to get more options and, therefore, more opportunity. Commercial lines lead lists are generally going to be smaller accounts, most likely newer in business. If you are pursuing larger commercial businesses, like big manufacturing outfits, it's important to note that accounts of that nature will not generally show up on lead lists.

Understand Exclusivity and Cost

There are several sources for lead lists, but not all are created equal. Getting a bargain on a list of 5,000 possible leads is not necessarily as good as it sounds. In other words, the deal may be too good to be true. Lead lists are often sold to multiple agencies, meaning that even though you have a lot of the necessary details, you will have to compete with another agency.

Obtaining a list that is exclusive, or at least semi-exclusive, may cost a bit more. But those leads will be more viable than the lower-priced leads, which are mass distributed. If the agency wants to generate revenue with less wheel spinning, spending a little extra on an exclusive list will be a far better route.

Establish a Process for Responding

Lead lists will serve no purpose if the agency does not have processes to handle them efficiently. When the lead calls or emails the office for more information, prompt response to the inquiry is critical, especially for lead lists sold to multiple agencies. Being the first to respond can make a tremendous difference in determining if the agency can secure the client before the competition arrives.

Setting up automated systems that immediately send a response to the prospect can be a game changer. You will be responding to the prospect when they are thinking about their insurance and reaching them before another agency has a chance.

Review Other Options

If your ideal client falls outside the area where lead lists are most effective, it's important to remember that businesses talk to one another. Your best bet on larger commercial clients or high net worth personal lines is going to be referrals. As you build successful relationships within your current book, there is a good chance they will gladly recommend your services should a friend, family member, or fellow business owner come looking for insurance agent recommendations.

The need for good leads is a valid concern for agencies and their producers to meet growth goals. Using the tips above, agencies can decide if lead lists are the right route for their organization.

45. How Do You Keep Your Team Engaged in a Remote Work Environment?

Our agency has decided to keep employees working remote. I lead a small team that handled working and connecting virtually for the first few months, but I'm now seeing a decline in morale and quality of work. Given that remote work is becoming the norm, how do I pull my team together and get everyone back on track?

Sending teams to work remotely in early 2020 sent a bit of a shockwave through the industry, especially for offices operating in a traditional brick and mortar space. When agencies had to pivot to virtual operations, there was an understanding that this would be temporary. While some agencies have started to move back to "normal" office environments, restrictions and precautions remain prevalent, leaving agency owners to decide what makes the most sense given legal and moral obligations. Teams that once shared a physical location had to adapt to new working arrangements. Many agents are genuinely concerned with the loss of the "team" feeling, which is growing the more prolonged the separation remains.

Knowing that a remote work environment may be necessary for a few more months, or potentially permanent, it is increasingly critical that leaders find ways to encourage individuals and teams who have lost momentum. Here are a few things to consider if you find yourself in this situation:

Check In Daily

While this may have been an area of emphasis initially, it is not getting the same level of attention now. It is easy to understand why this daily practice seemed more critical during the adjustment phase than it did a few months later. However, if you have noticed that employees are less connected and struggling with their work, reviving these daily conversations could make a significant difference.

When having these conversations, make sure that it is not just about work and allow them to open up about personal struggles that are impacting work. Check-ins give you an excellent opportunity to understand how the employee is managing both their workload and their emotions. It also demonstrates your continued investment in them despite the ongoing separation.

Get Creative

In a quarantined world, a lot of personal interactions are no longer available.

This loss of interaction can be challenging, both mentally and emotionally. Virtual meetings are the most effective option outside of the traditional face-to-face meeting. However, they only go so far. You may be able to cover a lot of work-related business during these video chats, but employees are likely missing personal connections that helped create a sense of comradery in the past.

To add some energy back to the team, provide opportunities for everyone to get together and talk about topics *other than* work. Gatherings like this are still an option even in a remote work environment. Utilize the same video conferencing technology used for meetings to host virtual happy hours. And if employees live in the same communities, the option to get together in a location where you can be face-to-face but still honor social distancing guidelines can be a fantastic option. If you aren't sure what to do as a leader, ask the team for ideas. They may very well have thoughts on what could help them feel more connected again.

Provide Flexibility

For your employees, losing their sense of control can contribute to their loss of morale and productivity. Most employees are experiencing many changes outside of work, which creates a sense of instability and insecurity. Many have found themselves trying to work and manage kids' activities due to a lack of alternatives. Trying to sort through constant change and distractions will undoubtedly start to impact focus and productivity.

Offering some flexibility that allows employees to regain some control may give them the boost they need. Allowing employees to choose different working hours to manage their professional and personal obligations more efficiently can help them regain their control and balance.

As the world continues to adjust and readjust, employers will need to do the same. Just as importantly, leaders must find ways to help their employees navigate a multitude of shifting stressors.

46. How Do Agencies Navigate Multiple Producer Compensation Plans?

Over the years we have brought agents in with a variety of different compensation structures. We've got upwards of twenty different agreements, and keeping all of them straight is a nightmare for accounting, managers, and anyone who enters commissions into the system. Can we remove these individual agreements and create more consistency? Is there a pay structure fee that works best for new business and renewals?

Producer compensation can be a sensitive topic with no perfect solution. Every agency seems to set these up in a unique way. Attempting to create the perfect formula for every producer can be a futile effort. Choosing the cookie-cutter approach rather than analyzing and evaluating each producer book based on individual merit can lead to frustration.

While the desire for simplicity and consistency can be a valid concern, a one-size-fits-all system does not necessarily work. Here are some things to consider before implementing significant changes to producer compensation structures.

Examine Specifics of Each Book

Some producer books are very niche specific, while others contain a more diverse set of business types. In the same regard, some books are very low maintenance, and some are very labor intensive.

The general level of service required for a book directly correlates to its profitability. A book that demands a high level of service requires a lot of backend work by an account manager to ensure the agency meets the leads' needs. Books of business of this nature tend to be less profitable. A lower renewal commission in a less profitable book makes sense, especially given that an account manager handles the service rather than the producer. However, those books that are lower in maintenance and higher in profit may validate higher commission splits. Evaluate the characteristics of each book and consider necessary modifications based on specific criteria like profitability.

Find Room for Consistency and Flexibility

Not all books are created equal. Attempting to fit all of them into one commission structure can be detrimental to the producer and, eventually, the agency. Modifying a well-established compensation plan in a way that reduces the producer's income can put the agency at risk of losing producers who can find a more favorable split elsewhere. Creating a compensation structure that is too rigid may also leave the agency unable to attract producers who are being paid better at their current agency.

If the goal is greater consistency, formulate a plan that works toward this moving forward rather than going and making changes that can generate negative consequences to the existing book.

Evaluate Technology

Managing multiple commission schedules for multiple producers can present a host of challenges, especially if the agency does not utilize the right software to manage the information.

If the system requires a manual, hands-on approach to keep commissions accurately coded, it is time for an upgrade. A more modern setup will manage new business and renewal percentages by producer and distribute those percentages through all AMS transactions. A system with these automatic defaults will reduce human interaction, human error, and human frustration involved in the process and should only require updating if the percentages ever need to be changed.

The need for consistency will always be front and center within the operations of an agency. Applying this to producer compensation may not be in the best interest of the agency or the producer.

47. How Should an Agency Handle Internal Moves?

I am part of the management team at a midsized agency. Employees are encouraged to apply for other open positions in the company. In the past, all managers were notified if someone from their team applied for another position within the agency. HR has now decided that this violates the employee's privacy, and their current manager no longer receives any sort of heads up. I think it has caused more harm than good, but what are your thoughts on internal moves in an agency?

As employees at your agency continue growing in their roles, they may develop an interest in finding out what else the insurance industry offers. When opportunities present themselves within the agency, opening those positions up to other staff may be met with resistance by some but can be an exciting possibility to others who want to explore new roles.

Here are a few things to consider when deciding how to handle internal moves in your agency:

Add Value for Employees

For employees who desire to continue building their insurance career, internal moves are tremendous growth opportunities. They may enjoy working at the agency but find themselves ready to move on from their current role. Such employees often desire to expand on their current skills and may even see a lateral move as a big step.

Opening a position to employees within the agency can mean that you are providing staff with opportunities and keeping them within the organization. It demonstrates that you care about and will invest in their continued success. Failing to open these roles within the agency can mean losing employees who will go elsewhere for new opportunities.

Ensure Employee Understanding of the Process

Whether applicants are from within or outside the organization, the agency should have a specified process. Making sure that employees understand the steps required of them throughout the application and interview process is critical. Also, clarifying upfront that there are no automatic guarantees they will get the position is essential. Overlooking or avoiding this detail could leave an employee bitter about the decision if they do not receive the job.

Communicate with the Current Manager

It may be difficult for managers to learn that someone on their team is looking to move on. However, creating an environment for open dialogue is critical. When good communication is encouraged, an employee will feel more comfortable having an open conversation with their supervisor. These conversations should allow the employee to explain their plans and why they are interested in another role. It is then up to the supervisor to handle the situation appropriately and encourage the employee's continued success. A negative or adverse response could be discouraging to the employee and undermine their confidence. If necessary, create a communication protocol that helps facilitate the conversation.

Create a Transition Plan

If an employee receives another position in the agency, they will likely be leaving a vacancy in their former department. Rather than leaving the employee to wonder when they will leave one position and start the other, it is vital to create a transition plan. Both the current and new manager should work together to decide on an appropriate start date for the employee. The hiring manager will need to make plans to hire a replacement and evaluate workloads.

If necessary, you can temporarily shift the employee's work to ensure that the agreed-upon start date is honored.

Allowing internal moves can present certain challenges but can be a great way to provide valuable employees with desired opportunities. The information above can help agencies prepare for these transitions.

48. When Should Your Agency Hire an Additional Team Member?

I am the CFO of an agency with about fifty employees between both commercial lines and personal lines departments. Both departments are submitting requests to hire additional staff, but when I look at the numbers, I think we're actually overstaffed. Do you look at revenue per employee when making staffing decisions? How else would you determine when it is time to add another person to your team?

Finding the right balance for staffing within an agency can be a struggle. Whether an agency is overstaffed or understaffed will impact the organization, and both can cause stress for different reasons. The numbers need to make sense, but looking only at dollars and cents may lead to inaccurate assumptions that bypass the agency's other needs.

Finding the right balance for staffing within an agency can be a struggle. Here are a few things to consider when deciding if it's time to hire:

Revenue Doesn't Tell the Whole Story

Depending on the organization's setup, there can be several administrative staff who don't directly contribute to the generation of revenue or the service of those accounts. However, those employees are still critical to the function of the organization.

Using revenue per employee is much more appropriate to benchmark against other similar organizations and ensure profitability remains within an acceptable range.

Consider the Impact on Morale

Running lean might appeal to you from a profitability standpoint, but it will not always be most beneficial to the agency in the long run. If an agency is understaffed, employees are overworked, or leadership must take on additional tasks to keep workloads in check, morale will quickly deteriorate. When employees experience this type of stress, they are less energetic and productive, which will inhibit your agency's ability to service current clients and bring in new ones.

Continuing to push forward along this path for profitability will eventually lead to unhappy employees who are burned out and leave the organization.

Understand the Reality of Time

The amount of work generated by a book of business will vary based on the type of accounts involved. It is essential to recognize that particular niches or specific accounts are more high maintenance than others. Accounts that require more touches and service will require more time from the employees who manage them. Also, some tasks take longer than others. Without understanding how long a task should take and how many times that task happens per day is necessary to understand individual workloads.

Consider Alternatives

The reflex to hire may seem like the most obvious solution when an employee's workload is rising significantly. However, filling a new position may not always be the right move. Once you evaluate how an employee divides their time each day, consider these other options before hiring:

- **Shifting workloads.** While one employee might be overworked, others may have more time left at the end of the day. Make sure to evaluate all employees who serve in the same role and consider moving a few accounts to balance things out.

- **Outsourcing.** If there is a significant number of accounts generating a high volume of non-client-facing tasks, investigate outsourcing as an option. Outsourcing behind-the-scenes tasks can provide a significant benefit to your employees who can then focus on work that is most critical to the client relationship.

- **Utilizing technology.** Certain tasks, like generating certificates of insurance, sending an email, or attaching documents to a client file, should happen with little disruption. If any of these tasks are lagging, the agency may have a technology issue. This problem could include storage issues, connection speed, or old software that can't keep up. Ensure you understand where tasks might be getting stuck due to technology and look into upgrades to speed these things up.

- **Training your current staff.** Understanding how quickly a task should happen and how fast an employee is completing it is critical information. Knowing this can help uncover struggles an employee may be experiencing. Identifying those areas where an employee is getting stuck will help identify the training needed to help staff become more efficient.

Knowing when and if it's time to hire can be a bit of a mystery. Using the information above, agencies can more clearly evaluate and identify when it's time to hire.

49. How Should Agencies Prepare for Retirement of a Key Employee?

One of our most experienced and well-liked commercial lines account managers recently retired. She was a longtime employee who built many of our most important client relationships. We're concerned about the impact her retirement will have on business and that some clients may leave. How do we address this with our clients and reassure them? When would you recommend letting clients know about future transitions?

It is common knowledge that insurance agencies and the whole industry will at times face massive waves of retirements. Many of these employees are leaving after thirty or more years of service at an agency and building relationships with clients. Not only does this mean that a significant amount of knowledge is retiring out of the industry, it can also leave client relationships in jeopardy.

And while there is no way to replace long-term experience, service, and friendships that an employee built, there are ways for agencies to prepare for their departure.

Be Proactive

While it may seem easier in the moment to bury your head in the sand and pretend one of the agency's most prized employees is not going anywhere, this type of mindset will not help anyone. Once an employee expresses a desire to start working toward retirement, it is time for the agency to start planning to accommodate this.

- Ensure that you are clear on the employee's plans, including the final day of work. This information will tell you how much time you have to start searching for and hiring their replacement.

- Get a full understanding of the particulars of an employee's book. Whether they are in a sales or service role, a long-term employee of the agency has a valuable relationship with clients. They may even be the reason clients have stayed. Understanding the full scope of the relationships within the book they work with is critical to knowing client expectations in the future.

- Hire the replacement employee with plenty of lead time. Creating an overlapping period before the current employee retires and the new employee steps into the role will significantly improve onboarding and training. The new employee may need time to learn insurance in general if they are new to the industry.

- If the new hire has insurance experience, they will still need time to learn workflows, the nuances of specific accounts, and a chance to get to know clients. Providing time for the current and new employee to comanage accounts will give clients necessary reassurance and make the transition much smoother.

Be Transparent

Employee retirements are not specific to the insurance industry, and businesses of all kinds are experiencing the same loss each day, just like your agency. Attempting to avoid the subject with clients does a disservice to them, the retiring employee, and the agency. Chances are, if the employee has a long-term working relationship with the client, the question of eventual retirement may have already come up in a conversation. Just as insurance agents want a heads-up when a client is transitioning from one key person to another, you now owe that same courtesy in return.

Be honest and communicate with the client about the timeline, the transition plan, and introduce the new service person. Open communication will allow everyone a chance to work collectively and get familiar with one another and avoid disruptions down the road.

It is understandably difficult to watch a good employee leave the industry for the next phase of life. However, using these steps will help position the new employee and the agency to pick up where they left off and continue building on their predecessor's successes.

50. How Do I Address Gender Discrimination at My Agency?

We have an agent in our office who is known for being extremely demanding with his account manager right down to telling her what to wear to client meetings. She has moved onto another role in the agency, and he has insisted on being part of the interviews for her replacement. The most qualified candidate was rejected by the producer as he did not feel she was attractive enough to deal with his clients. As the HR manager, I am appalled by this, but I am not getting support from any of the other managers. How do I address it?

The insurance industry has struggled with issues surrounding sexism for its entire existence. Insurance is a very male-dominated industry, with most leadership positions still held by men. Many agencies have operated with very traditional gender-specific roles within their organizations, while others have been more progressive.

Despite the significant improvement over recent years, there is still work to be done toward creating more gender equity. Here are a few critical tips agencies can utilize to move the needle forward:

Address Issues within the Agency

In some agencies, discriminatory language and behaviors are so typical that it has become normalized to most staff members. Women assume it is acceptable correspondence, and men in the agency feel it is acceptable to continue speaking the way they always have about colleagues of the opposite sex.

As common as this type of commentary may be in your agency, it is critical to address it once you notice it. Failure to tackle these types of conversations is ignoring harassing behavior. It is damaging to the agency's women and harmful to your reputation with clients and future employees. Instead, making a concerted effort to address unacceptable communication is the best way to rid your agency of it. To do this, agencies should:

- Develop a written policy regarding sexual harassment and discrimination and make it part of the employee handbook.

- Address organizational issues and changes with the entire agency.

- Ensure employees understand expectations and consequences regarding harassment and discrimination.

- Address specific problems directly with the individuals involved, clarifying expectations for what needs to change and outlining consequences if the behavior does not improve.

Review and Revise Agency Structure to Prevent Future Problems

While sexism is not exclusive to men versus women, it is more commonplace in arrangements where men and women work one on one. In other words, when a female account manager handles all of a male producer's book, it can lead to an unbalanced dynamic with the producer asserting an upper hand to the account manager.

To reduce issues at your agency and prevent future problems, shift accounts around. Require producers to work with a variety of account managers. Also, ensure that reporting lines are clear. It is understandable for a producer to request and expect account managers to meet clients' service needs, which gives the producer carte blanche. Any special requests outside of standard workflows or agency protocol should require a supervisor's approval rather than the producer's permission.

Advocate for Women in Your Agency

Communication is needed first and foremost to shine a spotlight on gender inequality issues in your agency and the insurance industry. Create a platform that fosters open dialogue to discuss problems females in your agency are experiencing in their work.

To ensure efforts, maintain momentum, recruit, train, and promote females into your agency's leadership positions. Provide opportunities for women in the agency to join the local community's leadership council geared toward women in business.

Combatting gender discrimination and harassment in insurance requires support from both men and women. Starting with the tips above can help your agency make great strides and elevate the conversation across the entire industry.

BONUS #1:
HOW TO SURVIVE YOUR FIRST 90 DAYS IN INSURANCE

"Your work is going to fill a large part of your life, and the only way to be truly satisfied is to do what you believe is great work. And the only way to do great work is to love what you do. If you haven't found it yet, keep looking. Don't settle."

— **Steve Jobs**

Starting a career in the insurance industry can be both exciting and overwhelming. Breaking down all you need to master into bite-sized pieces will allow you obtain the information you need and learn to apply it during the first year of your insurance career.

Insurance provides plenty of opportunity for growth and success in a variety of different roles. However, to build the career you desire, you must first learn the industry fundamentals.

Master the Basics First

There is always more to learn in the insurance industry, which is why you need a solid handle on the basics first. The basics are the building blocks for more complex concepts, and you' need a strong foundation to develop your career.

These quick tips will help you out in the early days, but they will also serve as helpful reminders in the future.

Learn the Language

Insurance has a very technical language full of confusing terminology, acronyms, and abbreviations. Not all of it will make sense right away, and that is perfectly acceptable. As you start working in the agency, you'll want to make note of new insurance terms as they come up in conversation. Write them down, look them up, read and reread the definitions to commit that information to memory for future use.

Follow the Processes

As you are working, you will quickly learn that the agency has established processes and procedures. A supervisor or trainer should be able to provide you with copies of the documented procedures in a binder or a video tutorial. As you go through these learning materials, note any confusing steps so you can review them with a coworker who is more familiar with the process. If the agency does not have a documented process, ask for screenshots of each step to utilize those when you are working on your own.

Tackle One Line of Coverage at a Time

There is a saying, "A mile wide and an inch deep," which means you might know a lot of little things, but there is no depth or substance to that knowledge. It is easy to fall into this type of thinking when looking at the variety of coverage and topics that exist within insurance.

Attempting to dive into too much at once will leave in the shallow end with very little to offer clients in the long run. Taking policies one at a time is going to be the most effective way to learn them. If possible, get insight from those around you with more experience as to which ones are the simplest, and start working your way into more complicated insurance subject matter as you build on that foundation.

Be Patient and Persistent

With so much to learn about the insurance industry, you won't wake up an expert after your first day. To master insurance, you need patience and persistence. Patience allows you to reduce the stress and be open to the learning and relearning process required in the insurance industry. Persistence will help you push forward through the setbacks you will experience throughout your career.

Acknowledge Your Limitations

Whether you are at the beginning, middle, or end of your insurance career, there will be times when you don't know the answer. It can be tempting in these situations to just make something up.

Not knowing about the topic at hand, however, can quickly lead to issues with the client. If you don't do your research, you may be putting a client at risk. Regardless, there is a significant chance you will have to go back to the client and retract incorrect statements. Having to do this can be embarrassing and damaging to the relationship.

"I don't know, but I'll look into it" is a much better answer. Make sure you have a complete understanding of the specifics the client has presented, and get to work digging into the question. If you happen to be right—great! You will have the confidence to answer the question the next time it comes up. If not, that is fine too. You have now learned something new and delivered accurate information to the client.

Know the Roles Inside the Agency

There are many roles in the insurance industry, even ones outside your agency. Understanding how each of these roles contributes to the insurance ecosystem will help you see how all the roles work together and help you identify where you fit into the picture.

First, let's explore roles within the agency.

Customer Service Representatives (CSRs)

This position is front and center addressing the daily service responsibilities within the agency. After an account is written, CSRs play a critical role in taking care of clients and retaining business for the agency.

If you are coming into the industry as a CSR, it's essential that you work cooperatively with others on your team, perhaps even training with one or more CSRs at the agency.

Others' experience can give you a clear picture of your role in the industry. Much of what they will cover is "textbook" information on coverage and workflows, but they will also can provide valuable insight about navigating client, carrier, and coworker relationships.

Within this group, you will want to seek out a key point of contact or mentor. This person will be someone you can go to for a variety of questions as they come up. Establishing the mentor relationship with another person in your department will carry you a long way as you continue to build knowledge and skills.

Producers

Producers focus on sales and therefore play an essential role in the ongoing growth of an agency by obtaining new business. Producers and CSRs will work closely together to support and build relationships with clients in the producer's book.

When joining the insurance industry in a sales role, you will quickly recognize that each producer has their own working style, and you will develop your own over time as well. Personality type and the makeup of your book will both contribute to forming a working method.

Relationships between Producers and CSRs are critical. Understanding each other's roles and establishing communication guidelines will play a significant role in creating a successful working relationship.

When this happens, it is easier to establish and build trust, which benefits the clients, and helps drive future success for the agency.

Management

Whether you are coming into an agency in service or sales, you will have a manager or supervisor you will work with, probably more frequently in the early days. Overall, management structures, however, will vary from one agency to the next and depend on the organization's size.

Your manager or supervisor will be a critical part of your success, so building a good relationship with this individual will be necessary. A manager will be the person who provides information about your role and responsibilities. They will also evaluate your performance, quality of work, and interpersonal skills with clients and coworkers.

A manager is also your advocate. Whether you have questions or concerns or need additional help, open communication with your manager to address these needs is essential so you can receive the support and guidance you need.

Know the Roles Outside the Agency

Next, let's take a look at relationships outside of the agency.

Carriers

The insurance carrier is the company providing the actual insurance policy. They are the company behind the product you are selling or servicing. In your role, you are the liaison between the carrier and the client.

Some of the people you will interact with at the carrier are underwriters or underwriting assistants, auditors, and marketing reps. Each of these people fills a different role in the agency-carrier relationship.

Underwriters and assistant underwriters review and evaluate client information submitted from the agency. They look at specific risk factors, rate according to those factors, and provide a quote back to the agency. Regardless of whether you are filing a sales or service role at the agency, you will want to communicate with them clearly and honestly. Ensuring that you are disclosing all client information pertinent to underwriting is critical to establishing trust and a healthy working relationship with the carrier.

Clients

The client is the customer and one of your top priorities in insurance. They are, after all, the ones paying the premium. Without clients, there is no need for insurance.

Client needs will vary by type. *Personal lines* focus on the needs of individuals and families, while *commercial line* clients need insurance for their businesses. Your role will typically support one client type or the other, though some agencies combine these roles.

Supporting these clients could mean addressing several different issues. Most of the time, however, clients will need information regarding coverage, premiums, billing, policy changes, or proofs of insurance like auto ID cards and certificates of insurance.

Invest in Relationships

Relationship-management skills will be critical to your role, and developing them early on will prove to be a significant benefit to your long-term success.

The demands of carriers and clients will vary. Carriers will expect complete information and prompt submissions and responses.

Clients will come to you with a variety of needs, but the key is always doing what you say you're going to do—and then working to exceed those expectations. If you say you will respond the same day, but then realize it will take longer to fulfill the request, it's essential to let the client know there have been delays, but also that you are still working on it.

Again, it's okay to let a client you don't have all the answers, but that you will work on their behalf to find them. "I don't know, but I'll find out" is a much better response than an inaccurate guess. Taking the time to get the right information will ultimately allow you to build a better relationship with the client.

The best way to build relationships is through effective communication. As you will quickly find out, there are several tools at your disposal to streamline communication. Most interactions will be via phone, email, texting, and face-to-face or Zoom meetings. Regardless of who you are you corresponding with, identify and become familiar with the method of communication most appropriate to the situation.

An email will be the most popular method of communication. It groups all of the correspondence in one thread and provides a way to document the conversation. However, even as convenient as email is, it is not always the best choice. When delivering difficult or complicated information, picking up the phone and having a conversation is going to be the most helpful. Sending an email with sensitive or complex information can offend the client or cause unnecessary confusion. Remember, a phone call allows you to make sure the client is clear on all the details and can always be followed up with an email to confirm the details.

Develop Effective Habits

Developing productive habits from the beginning will be essential to setting yourself up for success in the long run. It can seem like there is so much to learn and do, but putting the right practices into place will allow you to be more productive and effective.

First things first, you need to get organized. Creating and maintaining an orderly work environment is a great way to increase focus and keep your day on track. Ridding your desk of clutter and only the items you need to complete your work is a great way to reduce distractions.

Next, review projects and tasks each morning and start prioritizing. Prioritizing will ensure the most important items get done right away and are not at risk for slipping through the cracks. Taking time to itemize and prioritize helps you organize your day; you can also allocate time to each and block time in your calendar accordingly. It also ensures that you can move from one task to the next because you know what is next on the list.

Organizing and prioritizing your day from the start will also leave you better equipped to manage interruptions. Whether it is an urgent email from a client, a request from a producer, or a coworker stopping by, these are typical disruptions that occur every day. Knowing what you need to do and how to assess the priority of other items that come in throughout the day will enable you to keep your day on track.

Finally, scheduling your day will also ensure that you make time for breaks. Our brains need rest, and our eyes need a break from the bright computer screen. As tempting as it may be to do "just one more thing," recognize that stepping away will allow you to replenish and refresh so that you are ready to take on the rest of the day.

Stepping into the insurance industry can open a wide world of opportunity as you continue to learn and develop. Learning and implementing these basic practices will help you start paving a path toward long-term success.

Bonus #2
Becoming Indispensable

"Don't try to be the 'next'. Instead, try to be the other, the changer, the new."

— Seth Godin

Insurance offers unlimited opportunities when it comes to growth and development, career paths, and earning power. There is no other industry like it. The options for building a successful career in the insurance industry are endless, and you'll recognize this even within your first couple months. Once you've mastered the basics, you can continue building on those skills and apply that knowledge toward any industry segment that piques your interest.

The individuals who have found the most success in the insurance industry have found ways to add value to their organization and those they work with. Here's insight into how you can start doing the same.

Separate Yourself from the Crowd

Fine-Tune Your Processing Skills

When working in a servicing role, you will complete hundreds of tasks and microtasks throughout the day. Some tasks will be complex, and you'll need to spend time and effort to become comfortable and competent in them. Regardless of how easy or difficult a task may appear, it is essential to take the time to understand each part of the process. Attempting to speed through learning puts you at risk of making mistakes. As you continue developing these skills, you can start to put the pieces together and do your job more effectively.

Master Agency Technology

The technology in the insurance space continues to evolve quickly. For most of its existence, the insurance industry was technology resistant. However, a massive shift occurred with the emergence of insuretech, which encouraged those in all parts of the industry to rethink how they did business. Whether carriers, agencies, or shifting client expectations, technology impacts how this industry operates.

Over time, you'll certainly see the agency where you work adopting new technology. While many technologies may line up perfectly with agency functions, implementing new technology is a significant undertaking. New technology allows an agency to change how they do business and meet an increase in client demand for better and faster service. When agencies evaluate technology, they are typically looking for something that automates specific tasks, streamlines processes, drives new business, and creates an overall better client experience.

When it comes to your role and interaction with technology, taking time to build expertise in the tools you need to use will be a driving force in your success. Here are a few of the most common ones:

- **Agency management system.**
  The agency management system (AMS) will be the piece of technology you use the most frequently, so you'll will want to develop a thorough understanding of its functionality. Start with the parts of the system you use each day as part of your everyday process. As you master those areas, invest time in getting familiar with other parts of the system. Training videos from the AMS vendor will walk you through all system functions, taking you from a basic understanding to one that's more advanced. You'll learn how all parts of the system interact and impact the business.

- **Carrier websites and rating software.** As you begin to interact more with the clients and carriers, you will also be using the carrier websites more frequently. These websites will be an essential source of client information, including copies of policies, client billing information, loss runs, coverage forms, and more. As time goes on, you may also get a request to rate a policy online.

But no two carrier sites are built the same way. Take time to learn the nuances of the carriers you work with most frequently. When you can skillfully navigate these websites, you can rate coverage, get a quote, or locate client information quickly and easily. The more efficiently you can use the carrier website, the more effective you can be in your role.

- **Microsoft Excel.** Spreadsheets exist in all parts of the agency operation. They are critical holders of data output from the agency management system. Whether it is client data or agency reports, spreadsheets play an essential role in understanding the business. In your role, you will use them most frequently for various client data.

  Without proper knowledge, spreadsheets can be confusing, and Excel can be intimidating. However, it is an incredibly powerful tool that can provide great insight when appropriately used. Taking advantage of free trainings and building expertise so you can properly utilize the software will make your job easier and make you an incredible resource within the agency.

Being able to adapt to, learn, and gain proficiency in the technology the agency uses will be an excellent way to become an asset to the organization.

Strengthen Your Emotional IQ

Your emotional IQ, or level of emotional intelligence, is a critical piece of understanding yourself and relating to other people. Emotional intelligence plays an essential role in the interactions you have with people inside and outside the office.

Taking time to understand your current level of emotional intelligence and developing your emotional intelligence skills will positively impact your work. Here are options to help you expand this skill set:

- **Enneagram profile test.** The Enneagram profile provides insight into the nine different personality types. Completing this test will provide critical information about your traits and tendencies. You can also use this test to study other personality types and how you interact and respond to them.

- **Online courses or workshops.** Both of these options provide real-world scenarios and role-playing opportunities to practice utilizing your emotional intelligence skills. A simple online search will provide several options available free of charge.

- **Books, articles, and podcasts.** Whether you are a reader or listener, there is an option available and a wide variety of resources available through three mediums. Find an option that best compliments your learning style and dive in.

When this skill is used and improved, you become better equipped to manage the stress that comes with your role. It also helps you to tap quickly and easily into empathy when working with coworkers and clients. These byproducts will prove invaluable as you continue to grow in your career.

Enhance Your Problem-Solving Skills

Each day in an insurance agency is slightly different from the last, presenting a unique set of challenges that need attention. Challenges, both major and minor, will arise with clients, carriers, and coworkers, and you'll often have the responsibility of resolving them.

Problem-solving is the solution here and requires you use your critical thinking skills. Sharpening these skills requires practice. As you encounter problems throughout the day, evaluate the situation on your own before asking someone else for advice. Consider the desired outcome and the steps needed to make that happen. Once you have completed your analysis, discuss the problem and your proposed solution with your manager.

It will take time to build these skills, but it will prove to be an asset and provide you with a competitive advantage as your career continues to evolve.

Continuously Work on Your Coverage Knowledge

On day one, you'll see that there is a lot to learn about the insurance industry, and the best place to start learning is at the beginning. Start with the basics and be patient—you cannot possibly learn everything overnight. Beginning with a solid foundation of basic coverage knowledge is critical to being able to continuously build on that knowledge. Insurance concepts can be very complicated. Mastering the basics means you are equipping yourself with the information to decipher more complicated coverage situations later on.

To help with learning and retention of coverage information, consider these options.

- Create flashcards with new insurance concepts and terms. Study them and quiz yourself in your spare time.

- Use role-playing to think through insurance concepts and practice explaining them to a client.

- Research challenging insurance concepts. Discuss questions with carrier underwriters or claims representatives to clarify your understanding. They will often have valuable insight to share as to why and how coverage applies.

Investing time in gaining a real understanding of coverage will become more critical as you develop in your role. Be a student of the industry, and recognize the importance of improving your knowledge each day. A willingness to learn will allow you to expand in your role and add value for you, your clients, and the agency.

Master Workflows

Each agency has specific processes outlined for much of what you will need to do each day. Most of these processes take place within the agency management system and may seem cumbersome at first. Repetition will be the key to thoroughly learning and mastering each step of the workflows.

If recordings of processes are available to you, watch them, and follow along through each step. If recordings are not available, consider recording them on your own. Creating a recording gives you another chance to practice the workflow steps and creates a reference you can use in the future if you get stuck in the middle of a process.

The more you study and follow workflows, the easier compliance will get. Soon enough, the steps required will become part of the natural flow of your work.

Build Your Personal Brand

If you subscribe to any social media, you've already started building a personal brand. Your personal brand is a representation of you, and while it is separate from the agency where you work, it also intersects with your professional brand. This is important to keep in mind as you are posting on social media.

Brand-building is a form of marketing that helps generate brand awareness for you and your agency. This exposure can help create valuable connections throughout your community, leading to beneficial business relationships down the road. Finding ways to maximize and expand your brand presence is critical. There are several ways to accomplish this, but let's discuss some of the more popular options.

LinkedIn

You have likely used Facebook, Instagram, Twitter, and TikTok. LinkedIn is another powerful social media platform, but it was specifically so business professionals from around the globe could connect. As of 2020, LinkedIn has over 675 million members.

Members on this platform represent countless professions worldwide, including those within the insurance industry. LinkedIn is the best way for you to build a network of insurance professionals from all industry roles. You will find CSRs, agents, agency owners, educators, vendors, carrier underwriters, marketing reps, and many others. Connecting with these groups will allow you to get a better sense of the industry and all it offers.

Blogs and Vlogs

A significant part of building your brand is consistent interaction with social media. Two great ways to do this is through blogging and vlogging. Blogging focuses on delivering information through writing, typically around 500 to 1,000 words. Vlogging is merely presenting the message via video.

Both provide a great way to connect to an audience and share expertise. Understanding whether you communicate more effectively via writing or on camera will help determine which method will work best for you.

The most important pieces are delivering your blog or vlog regularly and ensuring that the content you provide is clear and relevant to your audience.

Articles

Another option to consider when working on building your online presence is publishing articles. An article, like a blog, is written content. However, articles are typically more formal and have more content, with a minimum word count of 1,500 words. Given the length of articles, it is critical that the topic remain relevant and that the structure appeals to your audience.

Associations

As you build your brand, you will want to ensure you make connections in the community where you live and work. Take some time to research business associations in your area. In most communities, you will be able to find industry-specific groups and other general business groups. Associations will typically have regular meetings and events. These events are a great way to connect with other professionals in your community.

When seeking insurance-specific associations, there are several options at the local, state, and national levels. These groups provide tremendous value from a networking and development perspective.

Volunteering

Addressing a volunteer need in your community is a great way to build your reputation and brand. The insurance industry is well known as one of the most charitable, professional groups nationwide. Many agencies have a philanthropic mission and support the causes their employees represent.

Find a local organization with a mission that aligns with your values and passions. There are plenty of nonprofits in need of time, talent, and financial resources. You will quickly find that giving back is rewarding work that also builds your brand.

Focus on Your Development

Putting time and effort into developing your role shows the agency you are committed to your continued improvement. When you are engaged and willing to continue learning and growing in your role, you become more skilled at your job, and the agency has an even more valuable asset coming to work with clients each day.

Performance Reviews

Continued growth and development is a critical component for building a successful career in insurance. Part of your ongoing development will be the performance review process. These meetings take place between you and your supervisor to provide feedback on your performance. Your agency may complete reviews on an annual basis or more often throughout the year.

Your supervisor will likely have a standard format they follow with specific performance criteria. During this time, your supervisor will supply feedback about your performance. This feedback will include things that you are doing well and those areas that need improvement. This time is also a great time to talk about growth and development goals with your supervisor. Whether there are other roles in the agency you are interested in or additional training or education you want, it is essential to discuss these topics with your supervisor. These conversations keep everyone on the same page and prompt your supervisor to help you formulate an action plan to achieve those goals.

While performance reviews might feel a little intimidating, they are incredibly valuable. Look at them as opportunities to have one-on-one time with your supervisor that you might not get very often elsewhere.

Promotions

As you continue to develop in your role, you may find that you're ready to take on additional challenges and advance your career. Be open with your supervisor about your career development goals and what you need to do to continue moving forward. Your supervisor should help by supporting your goals and guide you in the process, but you must be willing to take ownership.

You will need to work hard, accept feedback for improvement, and become a top performer. However, recognize that the availability of advancement may be limited depending on the agency's size. Promotions are also not guaranteed. These two factors should not stop you from working as if you're working toward a promotion, however. You need to ensure you are ready when the opportunity knocks.

Professional Designations

As you evaluate all the options available for continuing education, remember that the insurance industry allows agents to earn professional designations. An insurance designation signifies advanced education in a specific area. Most designations require an individual to complete a series of insurance courses and certification exams to earn the designation. Fortunately, options are abundant should you wish to pursue a professional designation. Courses cover a variety of topics with varying levels of difficulty, from introductory, intermediate, and advanced. As you continue your career, utilizing the educational resources available to you will challenge you, help you expand your knowledge, and make you even more of an asset to your clients.

A career in the insurance industry presents unlimited potential. Investing time and effort into your development will allow you to pursue opportunities, achieve great things in your first role, and beyond. As you lean into growth opportunities and challenge yourself, you will see the rewards of your efforts with a thriving career.